MyPlate Cook Book

ChooseMyPlate.gov

By Judy Doherty, PC II

50 basic lessons that teach everyone how to prepare quick, healthy meals.

foodandhealth.communications®

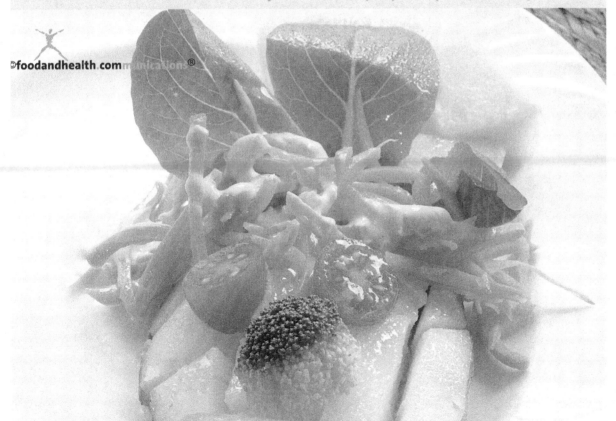

D0807522

MyPlate Cooking Demo Book

By Judy Doherty, PC II

50 basic lessons that teach everyone how to prepare quick, healthy meals.

For more cooking information, visit us online:
www.foodandhealth.com

Download our new Salad Secrets App for the iPhone for over 50 of our best salad recipes with photos - you can email them to clients right from your phone.

MyPlate Cooking Demo Book

Teaching modern cooking skills and MyPlate nutrition with delicious dishes in over 50 lessons.

Judy Doherty, PCII
Food and Health Communications
Louisville, Colorado
www.foodandhealth.com

Food and Health Communications

P.O. Box 271108

Louisville, CO 80027

www.foodandhealth.com

Copyright 2011 Food and Health Communications

All rights reserved.

Printed in the United States

This book is printed in ebook, epub, workbook and CD-ROM for-

mats. For special licensing, contact Food and Health Communica-

tions at 800-462-2352 or through

their website at foodandhealth.com

ISBN-13: 978-1466299719

ISBN-10: 1466299711

License to Copy

LICENSE TO COPY The Cooking Demo Book and Materials

PLEASE READ THE FOLLOWING BEFORE MAKING ANY COPIES OF COOKING DEMO II ("CDB").

As the original purchaser and current subscriber of Food & Health Communications, Inc.'s CDB, you are permitted to make copies of CDB, or any portion thereof, only (1) for your internal use or provision to your lay clients or patients, (2) for educational, non-profit purposes, and (3) for use at a single site. This permission neither transfers any ownership rights to you nor creates a relationship between you and CDB or Food & Health Communications, Inc. (Food & Health).

Without further prior written permission from Food & Health, you may not use CDB or any portion or copy thereof: for commercial purposes or gain; as part of another publication or work distributed for commercial purposes or gain; or for any other purpose other than as stated above. Without further prior written permission from Food & Health, CDB, or any portion or copy thereof, may not be distributed any further than as stated above, and no additional copies may be made.

Inquiries for such permission may be made to Food & Health at P.O. Box 271108, Louisville, CO 80027 or by calling 800-462-2352 or via email through foodandhealth.com.

You may not alter, edit, or revise any copy of CDB without the prior written approval of Food & Health. The changes in reproduction refer only to physical changes in our articles made in the reproduction process. For example, you can't "white-out" a name as author of an article, insert your own name, and photocopy the article. Changes in the way you actually use a recipe (for example, doubling the ingredients to allow for an increased serving size, or use of cashews instead of peanuts) do not implicate copyright law, and therefore are not prohibited by the federal Copyright Act or by the language of the photocopy language.

Each copy must include the relevant author's name and credits as originally provided in CDB, and must display the following notice in easily legible print on the first page of each copy:

© Food & Health Communications, Inc. www.foodandhealth.com.

The materials provided in CDB and any copies thereof are provided for informational purposes only. Neither CDB nor Food & Health makes any representations about the suitability of these materials for any other purpose. These materials are provided "AS IS," without any express or implied warranty of any type, and any individual or entity using these materials assumes all responsibility and risk for such use. Neither CDB nor Food & Health shall have any liability whatsoever for any use of these materials.

This book is dedicated to my son, Nicholas Doherty, who loves to cook in the kitchen with me.

If you'd like to cook with your family, here are some projects for kids.
- Two year olds can help set the table or stir lettuce in a bowl.
- Five year olds can assemble fruit plates.
- Ten year olds can be responsible for packing their own lunches every day.
- Thirteen to eighteen year olds can make dinner. After they learn to cook, let them plan and execute a meal entirely on their own.

If you start cooking at home more frequently while teaching your kids to help, you will find yourself with an able and enthusiastic sous-chef, a healthier child, more quality time with your family, a fatter wallet from reducing restaurant attendance, and better meals for all.

MyPlate Cooking Demo Contents

ChooseMyPlate.gov

Cooking Demo Success Tips

Choose the right recipe(s).
• Choose recipes that use the cooking equipment you already have and that appeal to your clients.

Purchase foods for examples.
• Choose packaged foods that are high in sodium and fat and discuss their dangers. This helps clients see how label reading and cooking are important for their health. It also entertains them while things are cooking.

Practice.
• Confidence is the KEY to success in any cooking demonstration.
• Practice the recipe on your family several times before going on stage with it.

Provide handouts.
• Give your audience handouts with recipes, cooking tips, and ingredient substitution suggestions.
• Encourage the audience to follow along and take notes while you demo the recipes.

Organization is indispensable!
• Double check the equipment and shopping lists to make sure you will have everything you need.
• Organize your work area before you start each demo. Items you use first should be closest to you.
• "Clean as you go" should be your motto.

Check the power before you start.
Make sure the power is hooked up correctly for your equipment. Test your set-up by running all appliances at the same time before you start. Insist on fresh batteries for your microphone!

Appearance is important.
Wear comfortable shoes and professional clothing. Here are a few tips and reminders:
  • Black pants and a white blouse or chef's coat
  • Your hair should be tied back or secured
  • Makeup should be kept very light
  • Only a minimum amount of jewelry
  • No nail polish
  • Have 2 aprons in case you spill something
  • Keep towels to wipe your hands
  • It helps to stand away from the counter

Prepare ahead.

ChooseMyPlate.gov

• Prepare all recipes as far ahead as possible.
• Chop all vegetables, measure all ingredients, cook pasta, etc.
• Some dishes that take a long time to cook should be made in advance for tasting purposes. Show how to assemble with a 2nd set of ingredients.
• An audience becomes very bored if they have to watch you measure all the ingredients.
• This strategy can also come in handy when you are limited on cooking equipment. If you want to make a pie but don't have an oven, you can bake one ahead of time and just show them how to assemble it in class.

Keep a sense of humor.
Not everything goes as planned and a good sense of humor can carry you through the unexpected!

Find a helper.
Have an assistant to help monitor the microwave and stove so you can concentrate on your presentation and questions.

Keep your audience involved.
Ask for volunteers to come up and help you with various steps. Make them wash their hands before they start. This adds a lot of fun and interest to your demo and people appreciate being included in the cooking process.

Show how a finished dish should look
Give great presentation tips such as sprinkling with chopped herbs or parmesan and using colors of veggies and fruits. We have provided garnish and presentation tips for every recipe leader guide.

Encourage questions at the end.
Take questions at the end while your assistant is dishing up samples. This helps keep your demo moving and prevents you from becoming distracted while trying to cook.

Be food safe
Follow the food safety tips in the Food Safety Lesson of this kit. When in doubt, throw it out.

Cooking Demo Food Safety Tips

Food safety is important when doing cooking demos. Usually cooking demos are done under less than ideal conditions- no sink, very little space, no refrigerator, etc. Here is a list of necessities:

____ Soap, nail brush, paper towels for handwashing
____ Trash bags for trash and dirty implements
____ Ice
____ Thermometers (liquids and meat)
____ Disposable containers
____ Portable sanitizer
____ Hot plate to keep foods warm
____ Separate utensils for raw and cooked foods

Review Cooking for Groups from FSIS:
http://www.fsis.usda.gov/Fact_Sheets/Cooking_for_Groups_Index/
Free PowerPoint on Cooking for Groups:
http://communicatingfoodforhealth.com/FREE-Handouts-and-More/Presentation-Ideas
These four rules of food safety are often challenged in a demo kitchen scenario:

1- Wash hands and food surfaces often.
• Don't depend on the site to have adequate facilities and supplies for handwashing, refrigeration and cooking unless you've checked it out.
• Wash hands before you start and often as you go; dry with paper towels.
• If you are using volunteers from the audience, make sure they wash their hands before starting.

2- Separate: don't cross contaminate.
• Have a separate set of implements for raw and ready-to-eat food: cutting boards, bowls, forks, knives, etc. The reason for this is so you don't cross contaminate cooked or cold ready-to-serve food with raw food. In a cooking demo, you are moving rapidly to keep your audience entertained. So even if you do have running water and adequate washing/sanitizing facilities, you might not have time to wash everything to serve the food on or keep track of all this. Placing items on trays is efficient to move them about.
• Emphasize to your helpers that implements for raw and ready-to-eat foods, as well as the foods themselves, are to be kept separate. Do not serve any food that gets contaminated.
• Bring plenty of paper towels and a couple big trash

bags. One trash bag is for trash, the other is for dirty implements. Paper towels are important for wiping your hands and cleaning up with.

3- *Keep hot food hot.* Cook or reheat quickly and maintain temperature.
• Cook and heat quickly and at the last minute. Do not allow foods to sit at room temperature.
° Room temperature is never your friend!

4- *Keep cold food cold.* Chill quickly and keep below 45 degrees.
• Bring perishable foods to the site in a cooler filled with an adequate amount of ice. Use a thermometer to ensure that internal temperature remains below 45 degrees F.
• Use a cooler with plenty of ice and a thermometer if you don't have access to a refrigerator. If you are using a refrigerator make sure you don't open the door too frequently, overload the refrigerator or leave the door open.
• Judging from conditions at your demo kitchen, you may want to serve food you prepared off-site under more sanitary conditions and just demo enough to show how it is done.
• Bowls of ice water are helpful for placing smaller bowls of food that you want to keep cold during demo and tasting.
• If you're slicing and dicing fruits, vegetables, etc., it is important to wash them well before the demo and transfer them on site in plastic bags. It is also efficient to bring prewashed and cut produce to the demo in zipped plastic bags.
• Hot plates are good for keeping hot foods hot - if you have electricity. Propane camping stoves or butane stoves are excellent if you do not have electricity. Consider renting these items.
• Bring a portable sanitizer for counters and other food contact areas. A pump spray bottled (labeled "bleach water") with 1 quart of water and 1 tsp of bleach works very well.
• Bring clean disposable cups, plates and/or serving utensils for serving "tastes" of your goods.
• Plan ahead for leftovers, particularly during warm weather. Before giving any away, ask yourself: can the recipient take it home quickly, can they cool it and keep it cool, will they reheat it?
• When in doubt, throw it out!

Make A Healthy Plate with MyPlate

- **Grains** – Eat about 5-6 ounces of grains per day with at least half of those being whole grains. Grain foods are those made from cereal grains: wheat, oats, corn, barley, bulgur and rye. One ounce is equivalent to:
  - 1 slice of bread
  - 1/2 cup cooked pasta, rice, cereal, etc
  - 1 cup ready-to-eat cereal

- **Vegetables** – Half your plate should be filled with fruits and vegetables at each meal. Get a variety of the five sub-groups: dark green, red and orange, legumes, starchy and others. One cup serving is equivalent to:
  - 1 cup vegetables (fresh, frozen, cooked, etc)
  - 2 cups leafy greens

- **Fruit** – Eat 1.5-2 cups of fruit per day, and stick to whole fruit as much as possible. Avoid fruit products with lots of added sugar. One cup serving is equivalent to:
  - 1 cup fruit (raw, cooked, fresh, canned, frozen)
  - 1 cup 100% fruit juice
  - 1/2 cup dried

- **Dairy** - Get about 3 cups of lowfat dairy each day. Avoid high fat dairy and the dangerous saturated fat it contains. One cup of dairy equals:
  - 1 cup milk
  - 1.5 ounces cheese
  - 1 cup yogurt

- **Protein** – This group includes meat, poultry, chicken, fish, nuts, seeds, and legumes. Most people need to eat about 5.5 ounces of protein each day. One ounce serving is euivalent to:
  - 1 ounce of meat, poultry, or fish
  - ¼ cup cooked dry beans
  - 1 egg
  - 1 tablespoon of peanut butter
  - ½ ounce of nuts or seeds

- Key Consumer Messages – Follow MyPlate's other vtial guidelines
  - Keep **portions** small and reasonable.
  - Choose **low sodium** options when selecting soups, breads, and canned/frozen foods.
  - **Drink water** instead of beverages that include lots of added sugar (soda, sports drinks, etc).

Amounts given are generalizedt. Personalize your plan at *www.choosemyplate.gov*.

© Food & Health Communications *www.foodandhealth.com*

—Rice Cooker

What is it? A rice cooker cooks rice automatically. You measure the rice and water into a removable pot, cover and place in the rice cooker stand and turn it on. When the rice is cooked it shuts itself off or goes to warm. The advantages are no attendance time, perfectly cooked rice, no worries about forgetting and burning the rice.

What do you cook in it? Most often, a rice cooker is used for simple rice dishes. But it can be used for more elaborate rice dishes, too.

Where do you get one? Most department stores and discount stores have them. Look for one that is a size that fits your family needs.

How do you cook rice in it? Usually you use 1-1/2 to 2 cups of water per 1 cup of rice. More water brings softer rice; less water, dryer rice. Different brands or types of rice will also cook differently. The rice should sit in the cooker, with the lid on, for a few minutes after the cooking time is finished. If you don't have a rice cooker you can use a covered pan on medium heat on the stove and follow package directions.

—Crockpot

What is it? A slow cooker or crock pot (a trademark often used generically) is a countertop cooking appliance that maintains a low temperature for many hours, allowing unattended cooking of beans, soups, chili, stew, and other long-cooking dishes.

What do you cook in it? Items that require a long cooking time - such as beans, split pea soup, chili, stew chicken is best cooked in a crockpot. You can also make applesauce that is just delicious!

Where do you get one? Most department stores and discount stores have them.

How do you cook with it? Usually you put items in the crockpot, cover and cook on low (for 8 or 9 hours) or high (for 2 to 3 hours). If you don't have one, use a covered pot on low heat on the stove.

Note: keep food safe. Always used thawed ingredients; keep all items that touch food clean; keep amounts of food and liquid correct for the size of the cooker; do not use for reheating; if power goes out during cooking, discard food. FMI see *www.fsis.usda.gov* and search on slow cooker.

—Microwave oven

What is it? A microwave oven is a kitchen appliance that uses microwave radiation to cook or heat food.

What do you cook in it? You can cook vegetables, fish and chicken uniformly and quickly. You can heat water for beverages and leftovers quickly. It is also great for cooking oatmeal or reheating soups.

Where do you get one? Most department stores and discount stores have them.

How do you cook with it? Items should be covered. Do not use metal in the microwave. Follow manufacturer's instructions. Many microwaves have buttons for preset cooking times and power levels and can be used to defrost food, bake potatoes make popcorn or cook fish.

Useful links
- *www.foodandhealth.com/blog/* for cooking tips, recipes and fun meal ideas
- *fda.gov* - for label reading guide
- *ChooseMyPlate.gov* - for more information on MyPlate

MyPlate Shopping List

Visit ChooseMyPlate.gov for a personal eating plan.

Vegetables - fresh, frozen, canned:

Get a variety:

_____ kale, collards, etc.
_____ lettuce, dark green
_____ spinach
_____ carrots
_____ pumpkin
_____ sweet potatoes
_____ winter squash
_____ corn
_____ lima beans
_____ potatoes
_____ canned beans
_____ dried beans, peas, lentils
_____ broccoli
_____ cabbage
_____ cauliflower
_____ celery
_____ cucumbers
_____ eggplant
_____ garlic
_____ mushrooms
_____ onions
_____ peppers
_____ tomatoes
_____ zucchini, summer squash

Fruits - fresh, frozen, canned, dried, 100% juice:

_____ apples
_____ bananas
_____ blueberries
_____ cantaloupe
_____ grapefruit
_____ grapes
_____ honeydew
_____ kiwi
_____ lemons/limes
_____ oranges
_____ 100% juice
_____ peaches
_____ pears
_____ pineapple
_____ plums
_____ raisins or other dried fruit
_____ raspberries
_____ strawberries
_____ watermelon

Grains:

Eat at least 3 ounces of whole grains each day.

_____ barley
_____ 100% whole wheat bread
_____ cereal, whole grain
_____ crackers, whole grain
_____ flour, whole grain
_____ oatmeal
_____ pasta, whole wheat
_____ pita, 100% whole wheat
_____ popcorn, low-fat
_____ rice, brown
_____ shredded wheat
_____ wheat germ

Dairy:

Choose dairy products that are low in saturated fat and a good source of calcium:

_____ fat-free, light yogurt
_____ nonfat ricotta
_____ fat free half and half
_____ plain low-fat yogurt
_____ skim milk

Protein:

Choose lean and get a variety:

_____ beans, dried or canned
_____ beef, lean
_____ black-eyed peas, frozen
_____ chicken, breast meat
_____ egg whites
_____ fish
_____ lentils
_____ nuts (also counts as oil)
_____ peanut butter
_____ peas, dried
_____ pork, lean
_____ seafood
_____ sesame seeds
_____ sunflower seeds
_____ tuna fish in water
_____ turkey, breast
_____ veggie burgers

Brought to you by:

_____

Miscellaneous:

Choose items that are low in saturated fat, trans fat, sodium and added sugar.

_____ baking powder and soda
_____ chicken broth, low-sodium
_____ chocolate syrup, light
_____ cocoa powder
_____ herbs, dried _____
_____ jam, light
_____ ketchup, no added salt
_____ light tub margarine no *trans* fat
_____ mayonnaise, low-fat
_____ non-nutritive sweetener
_____ oil, vegetable
_____ reduced-calorie syrup
_____ salad dressing, low-fat
_____ soy sauce, light
_____ spices _____
_____ spray oil
_____ tea
_____ vanilla extract
_____ vinegar, flavored

_____
_____
_____
_____
_____
_____
_____
_____
_____
_____
_____
_____
_____
_____
_____
_____

Handouts:
- MyPlate, Cooking Equipment Notes, MyPlate Shopping List, Recipe(s)

Label reading lesson:
- Compare boxed rice mixes to plain brown rice for sodium content.
- Calculate fiber added when using lentils and brown rice versus a white rice box mix.

Get Organized - To Do Lists:

What to do ahead of time:
- Copy all handouts.
- Measure and chop all ingredients. Place them in plastic bags or cups.
- Start cooking lentils and rice before class starts so the dish is ready shortly after students arrive. Start cooking the onions and olive oil on low. Arrange ingredients around the rice cooker so you can explain what went into it.

Start class:
- Greet the class and distribute handouts.
- Ask how many are familiar with brown rice and or lentils. Pass those items around.

During class:
- Explain the usefulness of a rice cooker and how to use one and what to use if you don't have one (more information is on the Rice Cooker Handout).
- Show the ingredients that went into the rice cooker.
- Demonstrate how to serve the lentils and rice on an attractive and/or colorful plate.
- Ask for volunteers to help serve and distribute the Lentils and Rice topped with carmelized onions.
- While people are eating, explain the MyPlate groups you are presenting (grains, protein, and vegetables) and give a brief overview of their uses and benefits. Incorportate the MyPlate handout.

Final question:
On mixed items, how do you know if you are making a healthy plate? If grains and protein are about half and half you are good. Fill half the plate with fruits and veggies.

Lentils and Rice

Ingredients:
2 cups brown rice
1 cup lentils
4 cups broth/water (use low-sodium broth)
Granulated garlic
Black pepper to taste

Directions:
Pour all ingredients into a rice cooker; cover; allow to cook until "warm" button is switched on - usually after 30 minutes. Fluff with a fork and serve hot. This dish is excellent with an addition of carmelized onions on the top (recipe below).

Topping: Carmelized Onions:
1 onion, sliced thin
1 tablespoon olive oil
Cook onions slowly in olive oil until brown in a nonstick skillet over medium-high heat.

Serves 8 or makes about 15 tastings. 260 calories, 1.5 g fat, .5 g saturated fat, 0 g trans fat, 0 mg cholesterol, 200 mg sodium, 50 g carbohydrate, 8 g fiber, 11 g protein.

Make It MyPlate:
- Large tossed salad and fruit on half the plate

Ingredient List:
Brown rice
Lentils
Water
Low-sodium broth (can be chicken, vegetable or beef)
Granulated garlic/parsley mix
Black pepper
Olive oil
Sweet or yellow onion
Optional: RiceARoni type box rice mix for label reading comparison

Equipment List:
Measuring cups and spoons

Knife
Cutting board
Rice cooker
Stove top burner (can use portable one)
Nonstick skillet
Cooking spoon
Serving spoon
Attractive dinner plate

Paper Goods and Misc:
Plates, napkins, and forks for tasting
Paper towels for kitchen cleanup
Baggies and plastic cups for ingredients
Cleaning supplies for kitchen sanitation

Rice Cooker Lesson

Handouts:
- MyPlate, Cooking Equipment Notes, MyPlate Shopping List, Recipe

Label reading lesson:
- Compare boxed rice mixes to plain brown rice for sodium content.
- Calculate fiber added when using lentils and brown rice versus a white rice box mix.

Get Organized - To Do Lists:

What to do ahead of time:
- Copy all handouts.
- Measure and chop all ingredients. Place them in plastic bags or cups.
- Start cooking chicken and rice before class starts so the dish is ready shortly after students arrive. Arrange ingredients around rice cooker so you can explain what went into it.

Class starts:
- Greet the class and distribute handouts.
- Ask how many are familiar with brown rice. Pass the bag of brown rice around.

During class:

During class:
- Explain the usefulness of a rice cooker and how to use one and what to use if you don't have one (more information is on the Rice Cooker Handout).
- Show the ingredients that went into the rice cooker.
- Demonstrate how to serve the chicken and rice on an attractive and/or colorful plate.
- Ask for volunteers to help serve and distribute the Chicken and Rice.
- While people are eating, explain the MyPlate groups you are presenting (grains, protein, and vegetables) and give a brief overview of their uses and benefits. Incorportate the MyPlate handout.

Final question:
How many food groups did we use today? How many servings from each one?

Rice with Chicken

Ingredients:
2 cups brown rice
4 cups broth/water (use low-sodium broth)
1-1/2 cups cooked, skinless chicken breast, cubed
2 cups frozen peas and carrots
1 teaspoon coriander
½ teaspoon chili powder
1 teaspoon cumin
1 teaspoon granulated garlic and parsley
Directions:
Pour all ingredients into a rice cooker; cover; allow to cook until "warm" button is switched on - usually after 30 minutes. Fluff with a fork and serve hot.
Serves 8 or makes about 15 tastings. Each serving; 200 calories, 2 g fat, 1 g saturated fat, 0 g trans fat, 5 mg cholesterol, 94 mg sodium, 39 g carbohydrate, 3 g fiber, 6.5 g protein.

Make It MyPlate:
Steamed broccoli or tossed salad plus sliced apples = half the plate.

Ingredient list:	Equipment list:
Brown rice	Measuring cups
Water	Measuring spoons
Low-sodium broth -	Cooking spoon
can be vegetable,	Rice cooker
chicken or beef	Attractive bowl for
Cooked chicken breast	service
meat, skinless	Cutting board and knife
Frozen peas and carrots	
Coriander	
Chili powder	**Paper Goods and Misc.:**
Cumin	
Granulated garlic and	Plates, napkins, and
parsley mix	forks for tasting
Optional: RiceARoni type box rice mix for label reading comparison	Paper towels for kitchen cleanup
	Baggies and plastic cups for ingredients
	Cleaning supplies for kitchen sanitation

Rice Cooker Lesson

Handouts:
- MyPlate, Cooking Equipment Notes, MyPlate Shopping List, Recipe

Label reading lesson:
- Compare plain brown rice with popular boxed rice mixes - find out how many more milligrams of sodium is in the mix.
- Read labels for the prepared salsa.
- Compare labels for tortillas - the sodium and fat content does vary considerably by brand.
- Explain that grains are important but you do have to be careful of added sodium.

Get Organized - To Do Lists:

What to do ahead of time:
- Copy the handouts you need.
- Start cooking rice before class so that it is finished shortly after class begins.
- Chop and measure all ingredients and place in plastic bags and cups.

Class Starts:
- Distribute handouts.
- Ask for 2 volunteers to help put ingredients in serving dishes and heat some for the taco bar.

Class:
- Talk about the MyPlate grains group - find out how many people ate at least one whole grain yesterday.
- Talk about the benefits of brown rice and explain how easy it was to make in the rice cooker.
- Have everyone come up and make their own taco.
- While everyone is eating, talk about MyPlate. See if they can guess which food groups they are eating in this dish. Are they in the proportions advocated by MyPlate?

Final question:
How many food groups did we use today? How many servings from each one? Veggies, beans, tortillas and rice. Add a colorful fruit like berries or melon on 1/4th of the plate.

Vegetarian Taco

Ingredients:
1 cup nonfat sour cream - put in serving dish
1 cup prepared salsa - put in serving dish
1 cup shredded romaine lettuce - put in serving dish
1 can beans - heated in microwave and put in serving dish
8 medium flour tortillas - heated in microwave and put in serving dish
2 cups frozen corn kernels - heated in microwave and put in serving dish
3 cups prepared brown rice from rice cooker (2 cups water, 1 cup rice)

Directions:
Assemble all ingredients listed above and present in small bowls with serving spoons.
Allow everyone to make their own tacos with the ingredients listed above.
Serves 8 or makes 16 tasting servings. Each serving: 456 calories, 4.5 g fat, 1 g saturated fat, 0 g trans fat, 0 mg cholesterol, 205 mg sodium, 71 g carbohydrate, 10 g fiber, 17 g protein.

Make It MyPlate:
- Add colorful fruit like berries.

Ingredient List:
Nonfat sourcream
Prepared salsa
Romaine lettuce
Canned beans (low sodium variety preferred)
Flour tortillas (large)
Frozen corn
Brown rice
Water
Optional: compare to tacos in fast food

Equipment List:
Measuring cup
Microwave
Rice cooker
Serving bowls (6) various sizes for ingredients
Serving spoons for ingredients
Serving platter for tortillas

Paper Goods and Misc.:
Plates, napkins, and forks for tasting
Paper towels for kitchen cleanup
Baggies and plastic cups for ingredients
Cleaning supplies for kitchen sanitation

Rice Cooker Lesson

Handouts:
• MyPlate, Cooking Equipment Notes, MyPlate Shopping List, Recipe

Label reading lesson:
• Compare boxed rice mixes to plain brown rice for sodium content.
• Calculate fiber added when using brown rice instead of a white rice box mix.

Get Organized - To Do Lists:

Aromatic rice varieties include basmati, jasmine, Texmati, Wehani, and wild pecan rice. Aromatic rice is a general term used for rice varieties that have a perfumed, nutty aroma and flavor. This type of rice is available in both brown and white versions. White rice has been stripped of its most nutritional parts - the bran and the germ. But even with that loss, white rice is one of the grains that is lowest in calorie density.

Pick one of the aromatic brown rice types mentioned above and prepare one or more for a class tasting. If you can have access to more than one rice cooker so they may be cooked simultaneously, that is great.

It is also helpful if you can pass out various packages of aromatic and brown rice for examination by attendees.

Follow package directions and prepare the rice in advance - it is wonderful if the aroma of the cooking aromatic rice fills the room while attendees are arriving. It will smell like you are cooking nuts or popcorn! And if you feel creative, you can even mix the rice varieties - we especially like to mix the Wehani with plain brown rice.

Distribute the MyPlate handout and the Grains handout. Rice is one of the least calorie dense grains and is very easy to prepare. Using a rice cooker or even cooking on top of the stove can be easy for anyone!

Aromatic Rice Tasting

Ingredients:
2 cups aromatic rice (Wehani)
3 3/4 cups broth/water (use low-sodium broth)
Granulated garlic
Black pepper to taste
Directions:
Pour all ingredients into a rice cooker; cover; allow to cook until "warm" button is switched on - usually after 30 minutes. Fluff with a fork and serve hot.
Serves 8 or about 16 tastings. Each serving: 173 calories, 1 g fat, 0 g saturated fat, 0 g trans fat, 0 mg cholesterol, 102 mg sodium, 35 g carbohydrate, 2 g fiber, 4 g protein.

Make It MyPlate:
• Large tossed salad, grilled chicken or fish, pineapple or other fruit.

Ingredient List:
Brown aromatic rice (basmati, jasmine, Texmati, Wehani, and wild pecan rice)
Water
Low-sodium broth (can be chicken, vegetable or beef)
Granulated garlic/parsley mix (we like Badia brand but McCormick is good, too)
Black pepper

Optional: RiceARoni type box rice mix for label reading comparison

Equipment List:
Measuring cups and spoons
Rice cooker
Fork
Serving spoon
Attractive dinner plate

Paper Goods and Misc:
Plates, napkins, and forks for tasting
Paper towels for kitchen cleanup
Baggies and plastic cups for ingredients
Cleaning supplies for kitchen sanitation

Lentils and Rice

Ingredients:
2 cups brown rice
1 cup lentils
4 cups broth/water (use low-sodium broth)
Granulated garlic
Black pepper to taste

Directions:
Pour all ingredients into a rice cooker; cover; allow to cook until "warm" button is switched on - usually after 30 minutes. Fluff with a fork and serve hot. This dish is excellent with an addition of carmelized onions on the top (recipe below).

Topping: Carmelized Onions:
1 onion, sliced thin
1 tablespoon olive oil
Cook onions slowly in olive oil until brown in a nonstick skillet over medium-high heat.

Serves 8. Each serving: 260 calories, 1.5 g fat, .5 g saturated fat, 0 g trans fat, 0 mg cholesterol, 200 mg sodium, 50 g carbohydrate, 8 g fiber, 11 g protein.

Make It MyPlate:
Large tossed salad or seasonal vegetable recipe and fruit.

Ingredient List:	Equipment List:
Brown rice	Measuring cups and spoons
Lentils	Knife
Water	Cutting board
Low-sodium broth (can be chicken, vegetable or beef)	Rice cooker
Granulated garlic/parsley mix (we like Badia brand but McCormick is good, too)	Stove top burner (can use portable one)
Black pepper	Nonstick skillet
Olive oil	Cooking spoon
Sweet or yellow onion	Serving spoon

Rice with Chicken

Ingredients:
2 cups brown rice
4 cups broth/water (use low-sodium broth)
1-1/2 cups cooked, skinless chicken breast, cubed
2 cups frozen peas and carrots
1 teaspoon coriander
½ teaspoon chili powder
1 teaspoon cumin
1 teaspoon granulated garlic and parsley

Directions:
Pour all ingredients into a rice cooker; cover; allow to cook until "warm" button is switched on - usually after 30 minutes. Fluff with a fork and serve hot.

Serves 8. Each serving; 200 calories, 2 g fat, 1 g saturated fat, 0 g trans fat, 5 mg cholesterol, 94 mg sodium, 39 g carbohydrate, 3 g fiber, 6.5 g protein.

Make It MyPlate:
Large tossed salad or seasonal vegetable recipe and fruit.

Ingredient list:	Equipment list:
Brown rice	Measuring cups
Water	Measuring spoons
Low-sodium broth - can be vegetable, chicken or beef	Cooking spoon
Cooked chicken breast meat, skinless	Rice cooker
Frozen peas and carrots	Attractive bowl for service
Coriander	Cutting board and knife
Chili powder	
Cumin	
Granulated garlic and parsley mix	

Vegetarian Taco

Ingredients:
1 cup nonfat sour cream - put in serving dish
1 cup prepared salsa - put in serving dish
1 cup shredded romaine lettuce - put in serving dish
1 can beans - heated in microwave and put in serving dish
4 large flour tortillas - heated in microwave and put in serving dish
2 cups frozen corn kernels - heated in microwave and put in serving dish
3 cups prepared brown rice from rice cooker (2 cups water, 1 cup rice)

Directions:
Prepare all ingredients listed above and set out in buffet. Allow everyone to make their own tacos with the ingredients listed above. Serves 8. Each serving: 456 calories, 4.5 g fat, 1 g saturated fat, 0 g trans fat, 0 mg cholesterol, 205 mg sodium, 71 g carbohydrate, 10 g fiber, 17 g protein.

Make It MyPlate:
Add fruit on 1/4th of the plate.

Ingredient List:	Equipment List:
Nonfat sourcream	Measuring cup
Prepared salsa	Microwave
Romaine lettuce	Rice cooker
Canned beans (low sodium variety preferred)	Serving bowls (6) various sizes for ingredients
Flour tortillas (large)	Serving spoons for ingredients
Frozen corn	Serving platter for tortillas
Brown rice	
Water	
Optional: baked tortilla chips	

Aromatic Rice

Ingredients:
2 cups brown aromatic rice
3 3/4 cups broth/water (use low-sodium broth)
Granulated garlic
Black pepper to taste

Directions:
Pour all ingredients into a rice cooker; cover; allow to cook until "warm" button is switched on - usually after 30 minutes. Fluff with a fork and serve hot. Goes great with grilled or baked chicken or fish.
Serves 8. Each serving: 173 calories, 1 g fat, 0 g saturated fat, 0 g trans fat, 0 mg cholesterol, 102 mg sodium, 35 g carbohydrate, 2 g fiber, 4 g protein.

Make It MyPlate:
Large tossed salad or seasonal vegetable recipe, grilled chicken or fish, and fruit.

Ingredient List:	Equipment List:
Brown aromatic rice (basmati, jasmine, Texmati, Wehani, and wild pecan rice)	Measuring cups and spoons
Water	Rice cooker
Low-sodium broth (can be chicken, vegetable or beef)	Fork
Granulated garlic/parsley mix (we like Badia brand but McCormick is good, too)	Serving spoon
Black pepper	

MyPlate Skillet Meals

Handouts:
• MyPlate, MyPlate Shopping List, Recipe

Label reading lesson:
• Compare the sodium and fat content between this meal (recipe sheet) and the boxed/frozen dishes from the grocery store.

Get Organized - To Do Lists:

What to do ahead of time:
• Copy all handouts.
• Measure and chop all ingredients and put into bags or plastic cups. Cook rice.

Start class:
• Give everyone the handouts. Ask how many of them like to cook Asian food at home. How many ate a whole grain yesterday?
• Introduce today's recipe and explain the health benefits of the foods it contains.
• Gather volunteers to cook and serve the rice - you will need one person for each task. Everyone should wash his or her hands before starting food preparation.

During class:
• Follow the recipe and have the volunteer cook the veggies in front of the class.
• Serve the food. While attendees are eating, review the MyPlate handout.

Final question:
Which food groups did we use today?

Make It MyPlate:
Add some fruit - the brown rice, veggies and eggs make up the whole grain, protein and vegetable requirement.

Egg & Veggie Stir Fry

3 cups cooked brown rice (2 cups water, 1 cup rice)
1 tablespoon canola oil
1 tsp chopped garlic
1 tablespoon grated fresh ginger
1 pound frozen mixed stir fry veggies (or use assorted fresh vegetables)
1 cup nonfat egg substitute
1 tsp sesame oil
2 tablespoons light soy sauce
Directions:
Cook egg substitute in glass bowl in microwave for 3 minutes. Chop into squares and reserve. Heat nonstick skillet over medium-high heat. Add oil and sauté garlic until nutty brown, about 1 minute. Add ginger and then stir fry veggies. Cover and allow veggies to heat through. Add cooked egg. Stir and season with sesame oil and light soy sauce. Serve hot over rice.
Serves 4 (makes 8 tastings): Each serving; 327 calories, 6.5 g fat, 1 g saturated fat, 0 g trans fat, 0 mg cholesterol, 376 mg sodium, 54 g carbohydrates, 6 g fiber, 13 g protein.

Ingredient list:
Brown rice	Glass bowl
Water	Microwave oven
Canola oil	Cooking spoons
Garlic - fresh cloves	Plate to show final
Ginger root	presentation
1 pound fresh or frozen	Serving spoon
stir fry veggies	Hand grater for ginger
Nonfat egg substitute	Peeler for ginger
Sesame oil	Rice cooker or pan to
Light soy sauce	cook rice
Optional: frozen stiry	
fry dinner mix for label	**Paper Goods and**
reading comparison	**Misc:**

Equipment list:
Measuring cups and spoons
Cutting board and knife
Nonstick skillet, lid
Stove burner

Paper Goods and Misc:
Plates, napkins, and forks for tasting
Paper towels for kitchen cleanup
Baggies and plastic cups for ingredients
Cleaning supplies for kitchen sanitation

MyPlate Skillet Meals

Handouts:
• MyPlate, MyPlate Shopping List, Recipe

Label reading lesson:
• Compare the sodium and fat content between this meal (recipe sheet) and the boxed and frozen pasta dishes found in the grocery store.
• Compare sodium content for various brands of pasta sauce. You can also compare sodium in various kinds of broth.

Get Organized - To Do Lists:

What to do ahead of time:
• Copy all handouts.
• Measure and chop all ingredients and put into bags or plastic cups. Cook pasta and drain in colander. **Note that one pound of pasta is called for here because you use 8 ounces for this recipe and 8 ounces for the Pasta with Sauce on the next page - this allows 2 different pasta dishes from one batch of cooked pasta. If you are making one recipe, just cook 8 ounces of pasta.**

Start class:
• Greet the class and distribute handouts.
• Ask how many like to cook pasta? How many ate a whole grain yesterday?
• Gather volunteers to cook and serve the pasta - you will need one person for each. Everyone should wash their hands before starting food preparation.

During class:
• Follow the recipe and have the volunteer cook the pasta in front of the class. This is the broth version, but there is alos a microwave version on the following page. We recommend demonstrating both.
• Serve the food. While attendees are eating, go over the MyPlate handout.

Make It MyPlate:
This recipe uses grains and veggies. Add fish or chicken and fruit to have a healthy plate.

Pasta with Veggies - Broth Style

ChooseMyPlate.gov

8 ounces whole grain pasta, cooked
1 tablespoon olive oil
1 teaspoon minced garlic
4 cups assorted fresh diced veggies: tomatoes, carrots, broccoli, bell peppers
low-sodium chicken or beef broth
1 teaspoon granulated garlic
1 Tablespoon fresh basil, chopped
Black pepper to taste
Parmesan cheese, 2 tablespoons (grated)
Directions:
Heat nonstick skillet over medium high heat. Add olive oil and sauté garlic until nutty brown, about 1 minute. Add the rest of the veggies and enough broth to cover the bottom of the pan. Cover the skillet and allow to steam until veggies are crisp tender and heated through, about 3-5 minutes. Season with garlic, fresh chopped basil, black pepper and Parmesan cheese. Toss incooked whole wheat pasta. Serve hot. Serves 4 (8 tastings): 289 calories, 5 g fat, 1 g saturated fat, 5 mg cholesterol, 115 mg sodium, 50 g carbohydrate, 3 g fiber, 11 g protein.

Ingredient list
Olive oil
Garlic
Assorted fresh veggies: ripe tomatoes, carrots, bell peppers, broccoli
Granulate garlic
Low-sodium broth
Fresh basil
Black pepper
Parmesan cheese
Whole wheat pasta - small shape like penne
Optional: boxed pasta mixes for comparison.

Equipment list:
Pan
Nonstick skillet - large - with cover

Microwave serving dish with lid
Stove burner
Microwave
Colander to drain pasta
Measuring cups and spoons
Cooking spoons
Serving plates (2)
Serving spoons
Knife
Cutting board

Paper and Misc:
Plates, napkins, and forks for tasting
Baggies and plastic cups for ingredients
Cleaning supplies for kitchen sanitation

MyPlate Skillet Meals

Handouts:
• MyPlate, MyPlate Shopping List, Recipe

Label reading lesson:
• Compare the sodium and fat content between this meal (recipe sheet) and the boxed and frozen pasta dishes found in the grocery store.
• Compare sodium content in various brands of pasta sauce.

Get Organized - To Do Lists:

What to do ahead of time:
• Copy all handouts.
• Measure and chop all ingredients and put into bags or plastic cups. Cook pasta and drain in colander.

Start class:
• Greet the class and distribute handouts.
• Ask how many like to cook pasta? How many ate a whole grain yesterday?
• Gather volunteers to cook and serve the pasta - you will need one person for each. Everyone should wash their hands before starting food preparation.

During class:
• Follow the recipe and have the volunteer cook the pasta in front of the class. There are 2 ways to prepare pasta with veggies and you are doing the micorwave/pasta sauce version for this class. The broth version is on the preceeding page - we do suggest doing both for this class.
• Serve the food. And while attendees are eating, go over the MyPlate handout and the Grains handout.

Final question:
The pasta and veggies and veggie sauce are grains and veggies. Add lean protein and fruit to half the plate.

Pasta with Veggies - Pasta Sauce Style

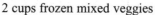

Ingredients:
8 ounces whole grain pasta, cooked (the other half from the recipe above)
2 cups frozen mixed veggies
1 26-ounce jar low-sodium pasta sauce
2 tablespoons Parmesan cheese

Directions:
Place all ingredients in large covered microwave dish, mix and microwave on high until heated through, about 7-8 minutes. Serve hot.
Serves 4. Makes 8 tastings. Each serving: 302 calories, 3 g fat, .5 g saturated fat, 0 g trans fat, 2 mg cholesterol, 225 mg sodium, 60 g carbohydrate, 6 g fiber, 11 g protein.

Make It MyPlate:

Add lean protein and fruit to half the plate.

Ingredient List:
Whole wheat pasta - small shape like penne or rotini
Low sodium pasta sauce
Frozen mixed veggies (peas and carrots are fine - can also use Italian mix or soup mix)
Optional: boxed and frozen pasta mixes and various types of pasta sauces for sodium comparisons - big difference with fresh made versus frozen or boxed!!!

Equipment List:
Microwave serving dish with lid
Microwave
Measuring cups and spoons
Cooking spoons
Serving plates
Serving spoons

Paper Goods and Misc:
Plates, napkins, and forks for tasting
Paper towels for kitchen cleanup
Baggies and plastic cups for ingredients
Cleaning supplies for kitchen sanitation

MyPlate Skillet Meals

Handouts:
• MyPlate, MyPlate Shopping List, Recipe

Label reading lesson:
• Compare whole eggs with nonfat egg substitute or egg whites. Note how the latter is much lower in fat and calories. Draw attention to the natural sodium content of egg whites - little sodium is needed when cooking with them.

Get Organized - To Do Lists:

What to do ahead of time:
• Copy all handouts.
• Measure and chop all ingredients. Place them in plastic bags or cups.
• Heat burner to low (if you're using an electric one).

Start class:
• Greet the class and distribute handouts.
• How many people had at least 2 cup servings of vegetables yesterday? This recipe is great for those looking for lowfat protein choices and more vegetables. It's also perfect for breakfast, lunch, or dinner. Ask for a volunteer to help you cook the omelet.

During class:
• Explain the importance of using oil sparingly - you can do that with cooking spray or by measuring oil by the teaspoonful instead of pouring it in the pan.
• Have the volunteer cook the omelet - you can guide him or her with the recipe directions. While he or she is cooking, you can toast the whole grain bread and cut the fruit (if you choose to use those accompaniments, that is).
• When the omelet is done, put it on an attractive plate and garnish with fruit and whole grain bread.

Final question:
How many food groups did we use today? How many servings (cups or ounces) from each one?

Make It MyPlate:
Add whole grain toast and sliced grapefruit or fruit salad to 1/2 of the plate.

Egg White Omelet

Ingredients
nonstick cooking spray
1 tsp minced garlic
1 cup mushrooms
¼ cup minced green onions
1 cup sliced zucchini or broccoli
3/4 cup nonfat egg substitute or egg white
granulated garlic
black pepper to taste
1 tablespoon parmesan cheese

Directions:
Heat a large nonstick skillet over medium high heat. Lightly spray with cooking oil spray. Saute garlic and mushrooms until lightly golden, about 2 minutes. Add green onions and broccoli. Add a little water and cover the pan until the broccoli is crisp tender. Add the nonfat egg substitute. Scramble briefly and then allow to cook into flat omelet. Turn the omelet when the bottom is brown. Season with garlic, black pepper and parmesan cheese. Serve folded in half. Serves 2 (makes 4 tastings): 91 calories, 1.5 g fat. .5 g saturated fat, 0 g trans fat, 2 mg cholesterol, 232 mg sodium, 6.5 g carbohydrate, 1 g fiber, 13 g protein.

Make It MyPlate:
• Whole grain bread, fruit

Ingredient list:	Spatula
Garlic cloves	Measuring cups and spoons
Fresh mushrooms	
Green onions	
Zucchini or broccoli	
Nonfat egg substitute or egg white	**Paper Goods and Misc:**
Granulated garlic	Plates, napkins, and forks for tasting
Black pepper	Paper towels for kitchen cleanup
Parmesan cheese	Baggies and plastic cups for ingredients
Cooking spray	Cleaning supplies for kitchen sanitation

Equipment list:
Knife and cutting board
Stove burner
Nonstick large skillet

MyPlate Skillet Meals

Handouts:
• MyPlate, MyPlate Shopping List, Recipe

Label reading lesson:
• Compare this frozen dinner with many of the boxed frozen dinners on the market. How many servings of grains, protein and veggies does each serving have?

Get Organized - To Do Lists:

What to do ahead of time:
• Copy all handouts.

Start class:
• Greet the class and distribute handouts.
• Ask who has ever made a frozen skillet meal? Is there anything that participants have done to make the meal healthier?

During class:
• Ask for a volunteer to cook dinner. Follow the directions for preparation on the package. Use as little fat as possible, and only use ¼ to ½ the sauce in the sauce packet. You can add a few fresh veggies or herbs if you wish.
• While the skillet dish is cooking, toss a large salad using packaged lettuce, fresh veggies, and flavored vinegar.
• Serve everyone samples of both the skillet dinner and the salad.
• While the group is eating, discuss the importance of limiting sodium consumption. Remind the group that MyPlate says people should "Compare sodium in foods like soup, bread, and frozen meals — and choose the foods with lower numbers."

Final question:
How can this dish be a part of a balanced, MyPlate meal? What would need to be added?

Bonus: Modify Frozen Skillet Meal

Many frozen skillet meals come with the sauce in a separate packet, leaving you with cooked noodles, vegetables and lean protein. By using just a little of the sauce instead of the entire sauce packet, you can end up with a dinner that is often lower in fat and sodium than most frozen meals.

Choose a variety of frozen meals and use their packages to illustrate how some choices are more adaptable than others. Usually the dinners with vegetables and chicken and a lowfat sauce are the best choices.

These can also be spruced up by adding more veggies and a few fresh chopped herbs for a "who would have known this was frozen" meal.

Ingredients:
Frozen skillet dinner with lowfat sauce in separate packet (do not choose alfredo or butter/cheese type sauces)
Cooking spray
Other fresh veggies
Ingredients for tossed salad
Examples of frozen dinners that cannot be adapted or are otherwise a poor choice because of fat or sodium content

Equipment:
Nonstick skillet
Knife and cutting board if needed
Stove burner
Salad bowl
Cooking spoon
Serving utensils

Paper Goods and Misc:
Plates, napkins, and forks for tasting
Paper towels for kitchen cleanup
Baggies and plastic cups for ingredients
Cleaning supplies for kitchen sanitation

Egg Fried Veggie Stir Fry

3 cups cooked brown rice (2 cups water, 1 cup rice)
1 tablespoon canola oil
1 tsp chopped garlic
1 tablespoon grated fresh ginger
1 pound frozen mixed stir fry veggies (or use assorted fresh vegetables)
1 cup nonfat egg substitute
1 tsp sesame oil
2 tablespoons light soy sauce

Directions:

Cook egg substitute in glass bowl in microwave for 3 minutes. Chop into squares and reserve. Heat nonstick skillet over medium-high heat. Add oil and sauté garlic until nutty brown, about 1 minute. Add ginger and then stir fry veggies. Cover and allow veggies to heat through. Add cooked egg. Stir and season with sesame oil and light soy sauce. Serve hot over rice.

Serves 4: Each serving; 327 calories, 6.5 g fat, 1 g saturated fat, 0 g trans fat, 0 mg cholesterol, 376 mg sodium, 54 g carbohydrates, 6 g fiber, 13 g protein.

Make It MyPlate:

This recipe uses grains, protein and vegetables so you should add fruit to 1/4 of the plate.

Ingredient list:	Equipment list:
Brown rice	Measuring cups and spoons
Water	Cutting board and knife
Canola oil	
Garlic - fresh cloves	Nonstick skillet, lid
Ginger root	Stove burner
1 pound fresh or frozen stir fry veggies	Glass bowl to cook eggs
Nonfat egg substitute	Microwave oven
Sesame oil	Cooking spoons
Light or reduced sodium soy sauce	Plate to show final presentation
	Serving spoon
	Hand grater for ginger
	Peeler for ginger
	Rice cooker or pan to

Pasta with Veggies - Broth Style

8 ounces whole grain pasta, cooked
1 tablespoon olive oil
1 teaspoon minced garlic
4 cups assorted fresh diced veggies: tomatoes, carrots, broccoli, bell peppers
low-sodium chicken or beef broth
1 teaspoon granulated garlic
1 Tablespoon fresh basil, chopped
Black pepper to taste
Parmesan cheese, 2 tablespoons (grated)

Directions:

Heat nonstick skillet over medium high heat. Add olive oil and sauté garlic until nutty brown, about 1 minute. Add the rest of the veggies and enough broth to cover the bottom of the pan. Cover the skillet and allow to steam until veggies are crisp tender and heated through, about 3-5 minutes. Season with garlic, fresh chopped basil, black pepper and Parmesan cheese. Toss in cooked whole wheat pasta. Serve hot. Serves 4: 289 calories, 5 g fat, 1 g saturated fat, 5 mg cholesterol, 115 mg sodium, 50 g carbohydrate, 3 g fiber, 11 g protein.

Make It MyPlate:

Add lean protein and fruit to half the plate.

Ingredient list	Equipment list:
Olive oil	Pan
Garlic	Nonstick skillet - large - with cover
Assorted fresh veggies: ripe tomatoes, carrots, bell peppers, broccoli, asparagus	Microwave serving dish with lid
Granulate garlic	Stove burner
Low-sodium broth	Microwave
Fresh basil	Colander to drain pasta
Black pepper	Measuring cups and spoons
Parmesan cheese	Cooking spoons
Whole wheat pasta - small shape like penne or rotini	Serving plates (2)
	Serving spoons
	Knife
	Cutting board

Pasta with Veggies - Pasta Sauce Style

Ingredients:

8 ounces whole grain pasta, cooked (the other half from the recipe above)
2 cups frozen mixed veggies
1 26-ounce jar low-sodium pasta sauce
2 tablespoons Parmesan cheese

ChooseMyPlate.gov

Directions:

Place all ingredients in large covered microwave dish, mix and microwave on high until heated through, about 7-8 minutes. Serve hot.

Serves 4. Each serving: 302 calories, 3 g fat, .5 g saturated fat, 0 g trans fat, 2 mg cholesterol, 225 mg sodium, 60 g carbohydrate, 6 g fiber, 11 g protein.

Make It MyPlate:

Add lean protein and fruit to half the plate.

Ingredient List:	Equipment List:
Whole wheat pasta - small shape like penne or rotini	Microwave serving dish with lid
Low sodium pasta sauce	Microwave
Frozen mixed veggies (peas and carrots are fine - can also use Italian mix or soup mix)	Measuring cups and spoons
	Cooking spoons
	Serving plates
	Serving spoons

Egg White Omelet

Ingredients

nonstick cooking spray
1 tsp minced garlic
1 cup mushrooms
¼ cup minced green onions
1 cup sliced zucchini or broccoli
3/4 cup nonfat egg substitute or egg white
granulated garlic
black pepper to taste
1 tablespoon parmesan cheese

Directions:

Heat a large nonstick skillet over medium high heat. Lightly spray with cooking oil spray. Saute garlic and mushrooms until lightly golden, about 2 minutes. Add green onions and broccoli. Add a little water and cover the pan until the broccoli is crisp tender. Add the nonfat egg substitute. Scramble briefly and then allow to cook into flat omelet. Turn the omelet when the bottom is brown. Season with garlic, black pepper and parmesan cheese. Serve folded in half. Serves 2, each serving: 91 calories, 1.5 g fat. .5 g saturated fat, 0 g trans fat, 2 mg cholesterol, 232 mg sodium, 6.5 g carbohydrate, 1 g fiber, 13 g protein.

Make It MyPlate:

• Whole grain bread, light margarine, fruit

Ingredient list:	Equipment list:
Garlic cloves	Knife and cutting board
Fresh mushrooms	Stove burner
Green onions	Nonstick large skillet
Zucchini or broccoli	Spatula
Nonfat egg substitute or egg white	Measuring cups and spoons
Granulated garlic	
Black pepper	
Parmesan cheese	
Cooking spray	

MyPlate Microwave

Handouts:
• MyPlate, Cooking Equipment Notes, MyPlate Shopping List, Recipe

Label reading lesson:
• Compare this recipe to regular canned minestrone soup. The canned stuff has about 960 mg of sodium per 1/2 cup (source: *campbellwellness.com*).

Get Organized - To Do Lists:

What to do ahead of time:
• Copy all handouts.
• Measure and chop all ingredients. Place them in plastic bags or cups.

Start class:
• Greet the class and distribute handouts.
• Ask how many eat canned soup on a regular basis.

During class:
• Pour all ingredients into a microwaveable container, cover and microwave on full power until the macaroni is tender, about 10-12 minutes. Stir occasionally.
• While the soup is cooking, review the MyPlate handout and/or make a salad to share with the class.
• Ask for volunteers to help serve and distribute samples for the class.

Final question:
How many food groups did we use today? How much sodium?

Mexican Minestrone Soup

ChooseMyPlate.gov

15 ounce can kidney beans, rinsed and drained
1/2 cup prepared salsa
1 cup corn kernels
2 cups low-sodium chicken broth
3/4 cup macaroni, dry
1 cup green bell pepper, diced
1 cup sliced cabbage
1 tsp dried oregano

Directions:
Combine all ingredients in a large pan or microwave container. If making on the stove, bring to a boil then reduce to a simmer and cook until macaroni is tender - about 15 minutes. Stir occasionally. If making in the microwave, cook on full power until macaroni is tender - about 12-15 minutes, stirring occasionally. Optional: garnish with nonfat plain yogurt and chopped cilantro or dried oregano.
Serves 4 (makes 8 tastings). Each serving: 230 calories, 1 g fat, 0 g saturated fat, 0 g trans fat, 0 mg cholesterol, 330 mg sodium, 41 g carbohydrate, 7 g fiber, 14 g protein.

Make It MyPlate:
This recipe uses vegetables, protein and grains so you should serve fruit to the side.

Ingredient List:	Knife
1 can kidney beans	Cutting board
1 can low-sodium broth	Pan
prepared salsa	Stove top burner
frozen corn	Cooking spoon
dry macaroni	Serving spoon
bell pepper	Attractive dinner plate
cabbage or slaw mix	
dried oregano	**Paper and Misc:**
various cans of soup to show sodium content	Cups, napkins and forks for tasting
	Paper towels for kitchen cleanup
Equipment List:	Baggies and plastic cups for ingredients
Measuring cups and spoons	Cleaning supplies for kitchen sanitation
Can Opener	

MyPlate Microwave

Handouts:
• MyPlate, Cooking Equipment Notes, MyPlate Shopping List, Recipe

Label reading lesson:
• Compare frozen fish dinners to this recipe. What is the fat and sodium content for each?

Get Organized - To Do Lists:

What to do ahead of time:
• Copy all handouts.
• Measure and chop all ingredients. Place them in plastic bags or cups.
• Cook yam in the microwave - it takes about 4 or 5 minutes or until fork tender.

Start class:
• Greet the class and distribute handouts.
• Ask how many people cook fish in a microwave. Explain that the microwave is actually excellent for cooking fish and chicken breast because these cook quickly and do not have connective tissue that requires tenderization.
• Point out that many of today's microwave ovens have a fish and chicken setting (along with other settings for foods like potatoes and popcorn).

During class:
• Place fish filet in a microwaveable container with a cover; microwave on the fish setting (or in 3 minute increments on medium power) until done. It takes about 3 minutes per fillet.
• Prepare salsa by mixing chopped peaches with prepared salsa.
• Toss salad.
• Cut yam in half and top with cinnamon and low-calorie maple syrup.
• Arrange an attractive plate with yams, fish topped with salsa, and a tossed salad. Show to the class and then cut up and put into sample cups.

Make It MyPlate:
Why does MyPlate recommend getting at least 8 ounces of seafood per week? This recipe uses fish, vegetables and fruit. Add whole grain corn tortillas to 1/4th of the plate for a complete healthy plate.

Fish with Peach Salsa

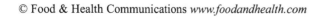

3 ounce fillet fresh or frozen fish - salmon, tilapia, snapper or grouper
1 Tbsp prepared salsa
1 fresh or canned peach, diced
1 yam
2 cups lettuce
1 cup assorted chopped vegetables
vinegar for salad
Directions:
• Place fish filet in a microwaveable container with a cover; microwave on the fish setting or for 3 minutes on medium power until done. It takes about 3 minutes per fillet.
• Prepare salsa by mixing chopped peaches with prepared salsa.
• Toss salad.
• Cut yam in half and top with cinnamon and low-calorie maple syrup.
• Make attractive dinner serving plate with yam, fish topped with salsa and tossed salad.
Serves 1, makes 4 tastings. Each serving: 344 calories, 1 g fat, 0 g saturated fat, 0 g trans fat, 5 mg cholesterol, 460 mg sodium, 66 g carbohydrate, 12 g fiber, 20 g protein.

Ingredient List:
Yam
Fish fillet, fresh or frozen
Fresh peach
Prepared salsa
Salad ingredients
Cinnamon
Low-calorie maple syrup

Equipment List:
Measuring cups and spoons
Knife
Cutting board
Microwave oven
Microwave dish

Mixing bowls (2)
Cooking spoon
Serving spoon
Attractive dinner plate

Paper Goods and Misc:
Plates, napkins, and forks for tasting
Paper towels for kitchen cleanup
Baggies and plastic cups for ingredients
Cleaning supplies for kitchen sanitation

MyPlate Microwave

Handouts:
- MyPlate, Cooking Equipment Notes, MyPlate Shopping List, Recipe

Label reading lesson:
- Compare frozen chicken dinners to this quick recipe. How do the ingredients stack up?

Get Organized - To Do Lists:

What to do ahead of time:
- Copy all handouts.
- Measure and chop all ingredients. Place them in plastic bags or cups.
- Heat the corn in a covered microwave container.

Start class:
- Greet the class and distribute handouts.
- Ask how many ever cook chicken in a microwave. Explain that the microwave is actually excellent for cooking fish and chicken breast because these cook quickly and do not have connective tissue that requires tenderization.
- Point out that many of today's microwave ovens have a fish and chicken setting (along with other settings for foods like potatoes and popcorn).

During class:
- Show the class the BBQ chicken tenders and explain that they cook very quickly in the microwave oven.
- Place the chicken in a microwave container in one layer with the BBQ sauce. Cover and cook on full power for 5-8 minutes. The chicken is done when it is firm to the touch and its juices run clear (when pierced).

Final question:
How many food groups did we use today? How many servings from each one?

Make It MyPlate:
Add a fruit garnish for 1/4th of the plate.

BBQ Chicken Tenders, Corn, Salad

1 package chicken tenders, 12 ounces
2 Tbsp BBQ sauce
1 pound frozen corn kernels
1 Tbsp light margarine
1 bag ready-to-serve (or 6 cups) lettuce
2 cups assorted chopped raw salad veggies
Flavored vinegar for the salad

Directions:
- Place chicken tenders in a single layer in a microwave container, drizzle with BBQ sauce, cover and microwave on full power until the chicken is firm in the center and cooked through, about 5-8 minutes.
- Heat corn in microwave and top with light margarine.
- Make salad and top with flavored vinegar.
- Serve all items on a large dinner plate.

Serves 4 (makes 8-10 tastings). Each serving: 287 calories, 5 g fat, <1 g saturated fat, 0 g trans fat, 60 mg cholesterol, 223 mg sodium, 38 g carbohydrate, 8 g fiber, 25 g protein.

Ingredient List:
1 package chicken tenders, about 12 ounces
BBQ sauce
Frozen corn
Light margarine
Lettuce
Assorted fresh vegetables for salad (carrots, tomatoes, cucumbers, peppers, green onions)
Flavored vinegar
Package frozen chicken dinner for label comparisons

Equipment List:
Measuring cups and spoons
Knife
Cutting board
Microwave
Cooking spoon
Serving spoon
Attractive dinner plate

Paper Goods and Misc:
Plates, napkins, and forks for tasting
Paper towels for kitchen cleanup
Baggies and plastic cups for ingredients
Cleaning supplies for kitchen sanitation

Mexican Minestrone Soup

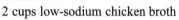

15 ounce can kidney beans, rinsed and drained
1/2 cup prepared chunky salsa
1 cup corn kernels, fresh or frozen
2 cups low-sodium chicken broth
3/4 cup macaroni, dry
1 cup green bell pepper, diced
1 cup sliced cabbage
1 tsp dried oregano

Directions:
Combine all ingredients in a large pan or microwave container. If making on the stove, bring to a boil then reduce to a simmer and cook until macaroni is tender - about 15 minutes. Stir occasionally. If making in the microwave, cook on full power until macaroni is tender - about 12-15 minutes, stirring occasionally. Optional: garnish with nonfat plain yogurt and chopped cilantro or dried oregano.

Serves 4 (makes 8 tastings). Each serving: 230 calories, 1 g fat, 0 g saturated fat, 0 g trans fat, 0 mg cholesterol, 330 mg sodium, 41 g carbohydrate, 7 g fiber, 14 g protein.

Make It MyPlate:
Serve fruit to the side.

Ingredient List:	Equipment List:
1 can kidney beans	Measuring cups and
1 can low-sodium	spoons
broth	Can Opener
prepared salsa	Knife
frozen corn	Cutting board
dry macaroni	Pan
bell pepper	Stove top burner (can
cabbage or slaw mix	use portable one)
dried oregano	Cooking spoon
various cans of soup to	Serving spoon
show sodium content	

Fish with Peach Salsa

3-ounce fillet fresh or frozen fish - salmon, tilapia, snapper or grouper
1 Tbsp prepared salsa
1 fresh or canned peach, diced
1 yam
2 cups lettuce
1 cup assorted chopped vegetables
vinegar for salad

Directions:
• Place fish filet in a microwaveable container with a cover; microwave on the fish setting or for 3 minutes on medium power until done. It takes about 3 minutes per fillet.
• Prepare salsa by mixing chopped peaches with prepared salsa.
• Toss salad.
• Cut yam in half and top with cinnamon and low-calorie maple syrup.
• Make attractive dinner serving plate with yam, fish topped with salsa and tossed salad.

Serves 1. Each serving: 344 calories, 1 g fat, 0 g saturated fat, 0 g trans fat, 5 mg cholesterol, 460 mg sodium, 66 g carbohydrate, 12 g fiber, 20 g protein.

Make It MyPlate:
Add a whole grain to 1/4 of the plate.

Ingredient List:	Equipment List:
Yam	Measuring cups and
Fish fillet, fresh or	spoons
frozen	Knife
Fresh peach	Cutting board
Prepared salsa	Microwave oven
Salad ingredients	Microwave dish
Cinnamon	Mixing bowls (2)
Low-calorie maple	Cooking spoon
syrup	Serving spoon
	Attractive dinner plate

BBQ Chicken Tenders, Corn, Salad

1 package chicken tenders, 12 ounces
2 Tbsp BBQ sauce
1 pound frozen corn kernels
1 Tbsp light margarine
1 bag ready-to-serve (or 6 cups) lettuce
2 cups assorted chopped raw salad veggies
Flavored vinegar for the salad

Directions:

• Place chicken tenders in a single layer in a microwave container, drizzle with BBQ sauce, cover and microwave on full power until the chicken is firm in the center and cooked through, about 5-8 minutes.
• Heat corn in microwave and top with light margarine.
• Make salad and top with flavored vinegar.
• Serve all items on a large dinner plate.

Serves 4. Each serving: 287 calories, 5 g fat, <1 g saturated fat, 0 g trans fat, 60 mg cholesterol, 223 mg sodium, 38 g carbohydrate, 8 g fiber, 25 g protein.

Make It MyPlate: Add a fruit.

Ingredient List:	Equipment List:
1 package chicken tenders, about 12 ounces	Measuring cups and spoons
BBQ sauce	Knife
Frozen corn	Cutting board
Light margarine	Microwave
Lettuce	Cooking spoon
Assorted fresh vegetables for salad (carrots, tomatoes, cucumbers, peppers, green onions)	Serving spoon
Flavored vinegar	Attractive dinner plate
Package frozen chicken dinner for label comparisons	

Slow Cooker Lesson

Handouts:
- MyPlate, Cooking Equipment Notes, MyPlate Shopping List, Recipe

Label reading lesson:
- Compare rotisserie chicken nutrition facts (*bostonmarket.com*) and frozen dinners or rice mixes for higher sodium content.

Get Organized - To Do Lists:

What to do ahead of time:
- Copy all handouts.
- Rinse chicken.
- Start cooking chicken before class starts.
- It is a good idea to make some of the 4 different meals from the chicken (4 recipes follow this one).

Start class:
- Greet the class and distribute handouts.
- Ask how many are familiar with using a crockpot.

During class:
- Explain the usefulness of a slow cooker and how to use one. You should also mention what to use if you don't have a slow cooker (the information is on the Slow Cooker Handout).
- Make one or more of the chicken recipes shown under accompaniments on the right side of this page.
- Demonstrate how to use a defatter cup to remove the fat from the broth.

Final question:
How much money does the chicken cost? Divide that number by four and you'll get the price per meal from a single chicken. How much money does one can of broth cost? We save that too, because this recipe makes broth as well.

Slowcooker Chicken + 4 Meals

Ingredients:
1 large whole chicken, defrosted and gizzards removed
Water to cover chicken
Bay leaf, black pepper, granulated garlic

Directions:
Pour all ingredients into a slow cooker; cover; cook on high until chicken is done and tender and the meat falls off the bone, about 3 to 4 hours. Allow the chicken to cool slightly, then discard skin and bones; cube the meat and package into 4 different bags for later use. Save the broth for later use - can be chilled and frozen in 1 cup portions in zip lock bags. See list below.

Suggested accompaniments: Make 4 different meals from the chicken, on the following pages, which include:
- Arroz Con Pollo
- Chicken Burritos
- Chicken Wild Rice Soup
- Chicken Veggie Stir Fry

Ingredient List:
Whole frying chicken
Water
Bay leaf
Black pepper
Granulated garlic
Optional: compare nutrient content with rotisserie chicken or frozen dinner package

Equipment List:
Slow cooker
Knife and cutting board
Defatter cup to remove fat from broth

Paper Goods and Misc:
Zip lock bags for chicken and broth (1 quart or 1 gallon size)

Slow Cooker Lesson

Handouts:
• MyPlate, Cooking Equipment Notes, MyPlate Shopping List, Recipe

Label reading lesson:
• Compare rotisserie chicken nutrition facts (*boston-market.com*) and frozen dinners or rice mixes for higher sodium content.

Get Organized - To Do Lists:

What to do ahead of time:
• Copy all handouts.
• Rinse chicken.
• Start cooking chicken before class starts.
• It is a good idea to make some of the 4 different meals from the chicken (see other recipes for details).

Start class:
• Greet the class and distribute handouts.
• Ask how many are familiar with using a crockpot.

During class:
• Explain the usefulness of a slow cooker and how to use one. You should also mention what to use if you don't have a slow cooker (the information is on the Slow Cooker Handout).
• Make one or more of the chicken recipes shown under accompaniments on the right side of this page.
• Demonstrate how to use a defatter cup to remove the fat from the broth.

Final question:
How much money does the chicken cost? Divide that number by four and you'll get the price per meal from a single chicken. How much money does one can of broth cost? We save that too, because this recipe makes broth as well.

1. Arroz Con Pollo

Note: this recipes uses the slower cooker chicken but is not made in the slow cooker.
Ingredients:
2 cups rice
4 cups low sodium chicken broth
2 tablespoons chopped green onion
1/4 cup chopped red pepper
2 tablespoons chopped sundried tomatoes
1/2 cup black beluga lentils (brown will also work)
1 cup cooked chopped chicken, skinless
Black pepper and garlic/parsley powder to taste
Place all ingredients into the rice cooker; cover and cook. 20 minutes later, dinner is done! (You can also cook on top of the stove and simmer all until liquid is evaporated and rice is done, about 20 minutes.)
Serves 6 (makes 12 tastings). Each serving: 339 calories, 3.5 g fat, 1 g saturated fat, 0 g trans fat, 30 mg cholesterol, 67 mg sodium, 60 g carbohydrate, 5 g fiber, 18 g protein.

Make It MyPlate:
Add a salad and fruit.

Ingredient List:
Brown rice
Lentils
Water
Low-sodium chix broth
Granulated garlic/parsley mix
Black pepper
Olive oil
Sweet or yellow onion
Optional: RiceARoni type box rice mix for label reading

Equipment List:
Measuring cups and spoons
Knife

Cutting board
Rice cooker
Stove top burner (can use portable one)
Nonstick skillet
Cooking spoon
Serving spoon
Attractive dinner plate

Paper and Misc:
Plates, napkins, and forks for tasting
Paper towels for kitchen cleanup
Baggies and cups for ingredients
Cleaning supplies for kitchen sanitation

Slow Cooker Lesson

Handouts:
- MyPlate, Cooking Equipment Notes, MyPlate Shopping List, Recipe

Label reading lesson:
- Compare rotisserie chicken nutrition facts (*bostonmarket.com*) and frozen dinners or rice mixes for higher sodium content.

Get Organized - To Do Lists:

What to do ahead of time:
- Copy all handouts.
- Rinse chicken.
- Start cooking chicken before class starts.
- It is a good idea to make some of the 4 different meals from the chicken (see other recipes for details).

Start class:
- Greet the class and distribute handouts.
- Ask how many are familiar with using a crockpot.

During class:
- Explain the usefulness of a slow cooker and how to use one. You should also mention what to use if you don't have a slow cooker (the information is on the Slow Cooker Handout).
- Make one or more of the chicken recipes shown under accompaniments on the right side of this page.
- Demonstrate how to use a defatter cup to remove the fat from the broth.

Final question:
How much money does the chicken cost? Divide that number by four and you'll get the price per meal from a single chicken. How much money does one can of broth cost? We save that too, because this recipe makes broth as well.

2. Chicken Burritos

Note: this recipes uses the slower cooker chicken but is not made in the slow cooker.
Ingredients:
3 cups cooked pinto beans, drained if using canned or boiled
1/2 cup prepared salsa
3 cups frozen corn kernels
2 teaspoons light margarine (trans-free)
1 cup cooked chopped chicken, skinless
1 cup fat-free sourcream
8 flour or tortillas, warmed in microwave at service time
Heat the pinto beans with the salsa in the microwave. Heat the corn with the margarine in the microwave. Allow everyone to assemble their own tortillas using beans, corn, chicken and sour cream.
Serves 8 (makes 16 tastings). Each serving: 311 calories, 5 g fat, 1 g saturated fat, 0 g trans fat, 22 mg cholesterol, 205 mg sodium, 50 g carbohydrate, 6 g fiber, 16 g protein.

Make It MyPlate:
Add some salad and fruit.

Ingredient List:
Brown rice
Lentils
Water
Low-sodium broth (can be chicken, vegetable or beef)
Granulated garlic/parsley mix
Black pepper
Olive oil
Sweet or yellow onion
Optional: RiceARoni type box rice mix for label reading

Equipment List:
Measuring cups and spoons

Knife
Cutting board
Rice cooker
Stove top burner (can use portable one)
Nonstick skillet
Cooking spoon
Serving spoon
Attractive dinner plate

Paper and Misc:
Plates, napkins, and forks for tasting
Paper towels for kitchen cleanup
Baggies and plastic cups for ingredients
Cleaning supplies for kitchen sanitation

Slow Cooker Lesson

Handouts:
• MyPlate, Cooking Equipment Notes, MyPlate Shopping List, Recipe

Label reading lesson:
• Compare rotisserie chicken nutrition facts (*boston-market.com*) and frozen dinners or rice mixes for higher sodium content.

Get Organized - To Do Lists:

What to do ahead of time:
• Copy all handouts.
• Rinse chicken.
• Start cooking chicken before class starts.
• It is a good idea to make some of the 4 different meals from the chicken (see other recipes for details).

Start class:
• Greet the class and distribute handouts.
• Ask how many are familiar with using a crockpot.

During class:
• Explain the usefulness of a slow cooker and how to use one. You should also mention what to use if you don't have a slow cooker (the information is on the Slow Cooker Handout).
• Make one or more of the chicken recipes shown under accompaniments on the right side of this page.
• Demonstrate how to use a defatter cup to remove the fat from the broth.

Final question:
How much money does the chicken cost? Divide that number by four and you'll get the price per meal from a single chicken. How much money does one can of broth cost? We save that too, because this recipe makes broth as well.

Make It MyPlate:
This recipe uses protein, whole grains and some veggies but you could complete it with a side of salad and fruit on a small plate.

3. Chicken Wild Rice Soup

Note: this recipes uses the slower cooker chicken recipe.
Ingredients:
4 cups defatted chicken broth from crockpot
1 cup brown/wild rice mix (if you don't have the mix, use half cup of each)
1/2 cup diced red pepper
1 cup chopped skinless chicken from crockpot
2 cups sliced fresh mushrooms
seasonings to taste: black pepper, garlic/parsley mix, thyme, Italian seasoning
Place all ingredients into a crock pot and cover. Cook on high power until the rice is tender, about 2 hours. Adjust consistencey with more water or broth as needed. We like ours thick.
Serve with a large tossed salad.
If you don't have a crockpot, simmer on the stove, covered, until the rice is tender, about 45-60 minutes. Add more liquid as needed, stir occasionally.
Serves 4 (makes 8 tastings). Each serving: 314 calories, 5 g fat, 1 g saturated fat, 0 g trans fat, 39 mg cholesterol, 60 mg sodium, 44 g carbohydrate, 4 g fiber, 24 g protein.

Ingredient List:
Brown rice
Lentils
Water
Low-sodium broth (can be chicken, vegetable or beef)
Granulated garlic/parsley mix
Black pepper
Olive oil
Sweet or yellow onion
Optional: RiceARoni type box rice mix for label reading

Equipment List:
Measuring cups and spoons
Knife

Cutting board
Rice cooker
Stove top burner (can use portable one)
Nonstick skillet
Cooking spoon
Serving spoon
Attractive dinner plate

Paper Goods and Misc:
Plates, napkins, and forks for tasting
Paper towels for kitchen cleanup
Baggies and plastic cups for ingredients
Cleaning supplies for kitchen sanitation

Slow Cooker Lesson

Handouts:
• MyPlate, Cooking Equipment Notes, MyPlate Shopping List, Recipe

Label reading lesson:
• Compare frozen dinners and canned mixes for higher sodium content

Get Organized - To Do Lists:

What to do ahead of time:
• Copy all handouts.
• Rinse chicken.
• Start cooking chicken before class starts so you can show them how to cook it and remove it from the pot and chop for later use
• It is a good idea to make some of the 4 different meals from the chicken (see other recipes for details).
• Have all ingredients chopped and stored in zip lock bags for class.

Start class:
• Greet the class and distribute handouts.
• Ask how many are familiar with using a crockpot.

During class:
• Explain the usefulness of a slow cooker and how to use one. You should also mention what to use if you don't have a slow cooker (the information is on the Slow Cooker Handout).
• Make one or more of the chicken recipes shown under accompaniments on the right side of this page.
• Demonstrate how to use a defatter cup to remove the fat from the broth.

Final question:
Which MyPlate food groups are used? Which types of veggies in the vegetable group play a role? Did we get something from all five vegetable subgroups?

Make It MyPlate:
This recipe uses protein, whole grains and some veggies but you could complete it with a side of salad and fruit on a small plate.

4. Chicken Stir Fry

Note: this recipes uses the slower cooker chicken but is not made in the slow cooker.

2 tablespoons olive oil
1/2 cup sliced carrots
2 cloves minced garlic
1 cup sliced mushrooms
1 cup sliced asparagus tips
1/4 cup sliced mild hot pepper
1/2 cup sliced red pepper
1 bag fresh snow peas
1 cup cooked chicken
seasonings: 1 tsp sesame oil, 2 tablespoons light soy sauce, 1 tsp ginger paste
2 cups cooked brown rice.

Pour the oil into the pan and heat over medium high. Saute the carrots then add the garlic, mushrooms, asparagus and peppers. Saute briefly until golden. Cover and stir frequently for a few minutes until crisp tender. Add the snow peas, chicken and seasonings and heat through. Serve w/ rice. Serves 4 (makes 8 tastings). Each serving: 176 calories, 6 g fat, 1 g saturated fat, 0 g trans fat, 39 mg cholesterol, 52 mg sodium, 8 g carbohydrate, 3 g fiber, 15 g protein.

Ingredient List:
Olive oil
Carrots
Garlic
Mushrooms
Asparagus
Hot pepper
Red bell pepper
Snow peas
Cooked chicken
Sesame oil
Light soy sauce
Ginger paste (or fresh ginger root)
Optional: Frozen stiry fry mix for label reading comparison

Equipment List:
Measuring cups and spoons
Knife
Cutting board
Slow cooker
Stove top burner (can use portable one)
Nonstick skillet
Cooking spoon
Serving spoon
Attractive dinner plate

Paper Goods and Misc:
Plates, napkins, and forks for tasting
Paper towels for kitchen cleanup
Baggies and plastic cups for ingredients
Cleaning supplies for kitchen sanitation

Slow Cooker Lesson

Handouts:
• MyPlate, Cooking Equipment Notes, MyPlate Shopping List, Recipe

Label reading lesson:
• Compare canned beans for sodium content.

Get Organized - To Do Lists:

What to do ahead of time:
• Copy all handouts.
• Start cooking beans before class. Then you can explain how to cook it then serve for tasting.

Start class:
• Greet the class and distribute handouts.
• Ask how many are familiar with using a crockpot.

During class:
• Explain the usefulness of a slow cooker and how to use one and what to use if you don't have one (on the Slow Cooker Handout).
• Explain how you made the crockpot beans and then serve them for tasting.
• It is great if you can serve brown rice and a tossed salad or slaw with this recipe.

Final question:
The beans fit into two distinct MyPlate food groups. Which two are they? (Answer: meat and vegetables). Complete it with a side of grains and fruit. We suggest brown rice and seasonal fruit salad.

CrockPot Ranch Beans

Ingredients:
3 cups water
1 pound dry pinto beans, rinsed, sorted
1 large onion, chopped
4 ounces cooked ham, chopped
3 cloves garlic, minced
1/2 cup chopped green pepper
1 tablespoon chili powder
1/2 teaspoon black pepper
1/2 teaspoon ground cumin
1/4 teaspoon dried oregano
Cover beans with water and soak overnight; drain. Place beans in a 5-quart slow cooker with water. Cover and cook on high setting for 2 hours. Add the rest of the ingredients and cook 1-2 more hours. Stir a couple of times during cooking and add more water if necessary.
Serves 8 (makes 10 tastings). Each serving: 225 calories, 2 g fat, .5 g saturated fat, 0 g trans fat, 8 mg cholesterol, 210 mg sodium, 37 g carbohydrate, 9 g fiber, 15 g protein.

Make It MyPlate:
• Serve with brown rice and a green salad or slaw.

Ingredient List:	Equipment List:
Water	Measuring cups and
Dry pinto beans	spoons
Onion	Knife
Ham	Cutting board
Garlic clove	Slow cooker
Green pepper	Cooking spoon
Chili powder	Attractive bowl
Black pepper	
Ground cumin	**Paper Goods and**
Dried oregano	**Misc:**
Optional: can of beans	Plates, napkins, and
for label reading pur-	forks for tasting
poses (higher in sodi-	Paper towels for
um)	kitchen cleanup
	Baggies and plastic
	cups for ingredients
	Cleaning supplies for
	kitchen sanitation

Slow Cooker Lesson

Handouts:
• MyPlate, Cooking Equipment Notes, MyPlate Shopping List, Recipe

Label reading lesson:
• Compare frozen dinners and canned stew with this meal. Which has higher sodium content? By how much?

Get Organized - To Do Lists:

What to do ahead of time:
• Copy all handouts.
• Measure and chop all ingredients and put them in zip-lock bags.
• Start cooking chicken stew before class starts so you can explain how to cook it, then serve for tasting.

Start class:
• Greet the class and distribute handouts.
• Ask how many are familiar with using a crockpot.

During class:
• Explain the usefulness of a slow cooker and how to use one and what to use if you don't have one (on the Slow Cooker Handout).
• Taste the stew. Have the class assist you with this.

Final question:
How many food groups does the stew use? Which ones?
This recipe uses protein and some veggies but you could complete it with a side of pasta and fruit on a small plate.

CrockPot Chicken Stew

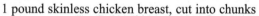

Ingredients:
2 teaspoon canola oil
1 onion, peeled and cut into chunks
3 carrots, peeled and cut into chunks
1 pound skinless chicken breast, cut into chunks
3 potatoes, cut into chunks
12 oz chicken broth
1 cup water
1 bay leaf
1 teaspoon garlic powder
1/2 teaspoon dried thyme leaves
1/2 teaspoon dried ground sage
Freshly ground black pepper to taste
Place all ingredients in 5 quart slow cooker and cook on high power for 2 hours or until potatoes are soft.

Make It MyPlate:
• Large tossed salad

Ingredient List:
Canola oil
onion
Carrots
Chicken breasts
Potatoes
Chicken broth
Water
Bay leaf
Garlic powder
thyme
Dried ground sage
Black pepper
Optional: Canned stew and frozen strew dinner for label reading comparison (higher in fat and sodium)

Equipment List:
Measuring cups and spoons
Knife
Cutting board
Slow cooker
Cooking spoon
Serving spoon
Attractive dinner bowl

Paper Goods and Misc:
Plates, napkins, and forks for tasting
Paper towels for kitchen cleanup
Baggies and plastic cups for ingredients
Cleaning supplies for kitchen sanitation

Slowcooker Chicken + 3 Meals

ChooseMyPlate.gov

Ingredients:
1 large whole chicken, defrosted and gizzards removed
Water to cover chicken
Bay leaf, black pepper, granulated garlic

Directions:
Pour all ingredients into a slow cooker; cover; cook on high until chicken is done and tender and the meat falls off the bone, about 3 to 4 hours. Allow the chicken to cool slightly, then discard skin and bones; cube the meat and package into 4 different bags for later use. Save the broth for later use - can be chilled and frozen in 1 cup portions in zip lock bags. See list below.

How it works:
Make 4 different meals from the chicken, on the following pages, which include:
• Arroz Con Pollo
• Chicken Burritos
• Chicken Wild Rice Soup
• Chicken Veggie Stir Fry

Ingredient List:	Equipment List:
Whole frying chicken	Slow cooker
Water	Knife and cutting
Bay leaf	board
Black pepper	Defatter cup to remove
Granulated garlic	fat from broth
Optional: compare nutrient content with rotisserie chicken or frozen dinner package	

1. Arroz Con Pollo

ChooseMyPlate.gov

Note: this recipes uses the slower cooker chicken but is not made in the slow cooker.
Ingredients:
2 cups rice
4 cups low sodium chicken broth
2 tablespoons chopped green onion
1/4 cup chopped red pepper
2 tablespoons chopped sundried tomatoes
1/2 cup black beluga lentils (brown will also work)
1 cup cooked chopped chicken, skinless
Black pepper and garlic/parsley powder to taste
Place all ingredients into the rice cooker; cover and cook. 20 minutes later, dinner is done! (You can also cook on top of the stove and simmer all until liquid is evaporated and rice is done, about 20 minutes.)
Serves 6. Each serving: 339 calories, 3.5 g fat, 1 g saturated fat, 0 g trans fat, 30 mg cholesterol, 67 mg sodium, 60 g carbohydrate, 5 g fiber, 18 g protein.

Make It MyPlate:
Add a side dish of salad and fruit.

Ingredient List:	Equipment List:
Brown rice	Measuring cups and
Lentils	spoons
Water	Knife
Low-sodium chix broth	Cutting board
Granulated garlic/parsley mix (we like Badia brand but McCormick is good, too)	Rice cooker
	Stove top burner (can
Black pepper	use portable one)
Olive oil	Nonstick skillet
Sweet or yellow onion	Cooking spoon
Optional: RiceARoni type box rice mix for label reading	Serving spoon

2. Chicken Burritos

Note: this recipes uses the slower cooker chicken but is not made in the slow cooker.

ChooseMyPlate.gov

Ingredients:

3 cups cooked pinto beans, drained if using canned or boiled
1/2 cup prepared salsa
3 cups frozen corn kernels
2 teaspoons light margarine (trans-free)
1 cup cooked chopped chicken, skinless
1 cup fat-free sourcream
8 flour or tortillas, warmed in microwave at service time

Heat the pinto beans with the salsa in the microwave. Heat the corn with the margarine in the microwave. Allow everyone to assemble their own tortillas using beans, corn, chicken and sour cream.

Serves 8. Each serving: 311 calories, 5 g fat, 1 g saturated fat, 0 g trans fat, 22 mg cholesterol, 205 mg sodium, 50 g carbohydrate, 6 g fiber, 16 g protein.

Make It MyPlate:
Add a salad and some fruit.

Ingredient List:	Equipment List:
Brown rice	Measuring cups and
Lentils	spoons
Water	Knife
Low-sodium broth (can	Cutting board
be chicken, vegetable	Rice cooker
or beef)	Stove top burner (can
Granulated garlic/pars-	use portable one)
ley mix (we like Badia	Nonstick skillet
brand but McCormick	Cooking spoon
is good, too)	Serving spoon
Black pepper	
Olive oil	
Sweet or yellow onion	
Optional: RiceARoni	
type box rice mix for	
label reading	

3. Chicken Wild Rice Soup

Note: this recipes uses the slower cooker chicken recipe.

ChooseMyPlate.gov

Ingredients:

4 cups defatted chicken broth from crockpot
1 cup brown/wild rice mix (if you don't have the mix, use half cup of each)
1/2 cup diced red pepper
1 cup chopped skinless chicken from crockpot
2 cups sliced fresh mushrooms
seasonings to taste: black pepper, garlic/parsley mix, thyme, Italian seasoning

Place all ingredients into a crock pot and cover. Cook on high power until the rice is tender, about 2 hours. Adjust consistencey with more water or broth as needed. We like ours thick.
Serve with a large tossed salad.
If you don't have a crockpot, simmer on the stove, covered, until the rice is tender, about 45-60 minutes. Add more liquid as needed, stir occasionally.

Serves 4. Each serving: 314 calories, 5 g fat, 1 g saturated fat, 0 g trans fat, 39 mg cholesterol, 60 mg sodium, 44 g carbohydrate, 4 g fiber, 24 g protein.

Make It MyPlate:
Add a side plate with salad and fruit.

Ingredient List:	Equipment List:
Brown rice	Measuring cups and
Lentils	spoons
Water	Knife
Low-sodium broth (can	Cutting board
be chicken, vegetable	Rice cooker
or beef)	Stove top burner (can
Granulated garlic/pars-	use portable one)
ley mix (we like Badia	Nonstick skillet
brand but McCormick	Cooking spoon
is good, too)	Serving spoon
Black pepper	
Olive oil	
Sweet or yellow onion	
Optional: RiceARoni	
type box rice mix for	
label reading	

4. Chicken Stir Fry

Note: this recipes uses the slower cooker chicken but is made in a skillets.

2 tablespoons olive oil
1/2 cup sliced carrots
2 cloves minced garlic
1 cup sliced mushrooms
1 cup sliced asparagus tips
1/4 cup sliced mild hot pepper
1/2 cup sliced red pepper
1 bag fresh snow peas
1 cup cooked chicken
seasonings: 1 tsp sesame oil, 2 tablespoons light soy sauce, 1 tsp ginger paste
2 cups cooked brown rice.

Pour the oil into the pan and heat over medium high. Saute the carrots then add the garlic, mushrooms, asparagus and peppers. Saute briefly until golden. Cover and stir frequently for a few minutes until crisp tender. Add the snow peas, chicken and seasonings and heat through. Serve w/ rice. Serves 4. Each serving: 176 calories, 6 g fat, 1 g saturated fat, 0 g trans fat, 39 mg cholesterol, 52 mg sodium, 8 g carbohydrate, 3 g fiber, 15 g protein.

Make It MyPlate:
Add a side plate with fruit.

Ingredient List:	Equipment List:
Olive oil	Measuring cups and spoons
Carrots	Knife
Garlic	Cutting board
Mushrooms	Slow cooker
Asparagus	Stove top burner (can use portable one)
Hot pepper	Nonstick skillet
Red bell pepper	Cooking spoon
Snow peas	Serving spoon
Cooked chicken	
Sesame oil	
Light soy sauce	
Ginger paste (or fresh ginger root)	
Optional: Frozen stiry fry mix for label reading comparison	

CrockPot Ranch Beans

Ingredients:

3 cups water

1 pound dry pinto beans, rinsed, sorted

1 large onion, chopped

4 ounces cooked ham, chopped

3 cloves garlic, minced

1/2 cup chopped green pepper

1 tablespoon chili powder

1/2 teaspoon black pepper

1/2 teaspoon ground cumin

1/4 teaspoon dried oregano

Cover beans with water and soak overnight; drain. Place beans in a 5-quart slow cooker with water. Cover and cook on high setting for 2 hours. Add the rest of the ingredients and cook 1-2 more hours. Stir a couple of times during cooking and add more water if necessary.

Serves 8 to 10.

ChooseMyPlate.gov

Make It MyPlate:

• Serve with brown rice, more veggies like slaw and fruit.

Ingredient List:	Equipment List:
Water	Measuring cups and spoons
Dry pinto beans	Knife
Onion	Cutting board
Ham	Slow cooker
Garlic clove	Cooking spoon
Green pepper	Attractive bowl
Chili powder	
Black pepper	**Paper Goods and Misc:**
Ground cumin	Plates, napkins, and forks for tasting
Dried oregano	
Optional: can of beans for label reading purposes (higher in sodium)	Paper towels for kitchen cleanup
	Baggies and plastic cups for ingredients
	Cleaning supplies for kitchen sanitation

CrockPot Chicken Stew

Ingredients:

2 teaspoon canola oil

1 onion, peeled and cut into chunks

3 carrots, peeled and cut into chunks

1 pound skinless chicken breast, cut into chunks

3 potatoes, cut into chunks

12 oz chicken broth

1 cup water

1 bay leaf

1 teaspoon garlic powder

1/2 teaspoon dried thyme leaves

1/2 teaspoon dried ground sage

Freshly ground black pepper to taste

Place all ingredients in 5 quart slow cooker and cook on high power for 2 hours or until potatoes are soft.

ChooseMyPlate.gov

Make It MyPlate:

This recipe uses chicken and veggies. Add a side of grains and fruit.

Ingredient List:	Equipment List:
Canola oil	Measuring cups and spoons
onion	Knife
Carrots	Cutting board
Chicken breasts	Slow cooker
Potatoes	Cooking spoon
Chicken broth	Serving spoon
Water	Attractive dinner bowl
Bay leaf	
Garlic powder	**Paper Goods and Misc:**
thyme	Plates, napkins, and forks for tasting
Dried ground sage	
Black pepper	Paper towels for kitchen cleanup
Optional: Canned stew and frozen strew dinner for label reading comparison (higher in fat and sodium)	Baggies and plastic cups for ingredients
	Cleaning supplies for kitchen sanitation

Fun with Half the Plate

Handouts:
- MyPlate, MyPlate Shopping List

Label reading lesson:
- When selecting frozen or canned options, heed My-Plate's advice and compare the sodium content in a variety of brands, then choose the option with the lowest sodium. This also applies to added sugars.
- You can also avoid labels completely and shoot for fresh, whole fruits and veggies when possible.

Get Organized - To Do Lists:

What to do ahead of time:
- Copy all handouts.
- Measure and chop all ingredients. Place them in plastic bags or cups.

Start class:
- Greet the class and distribute handouts.
- Ask how many people in the group are familiar with MyPlate's call to make half their plates full of fruits and veggies at each meal.

During class:
- Explain the importance of getting enough fruits and vegetables every day.
- Repeat this advice from the Dietary Guidelines for Americans, "A healthy eating pattern limits intake of sodium, solid fats, added sugars, and refined grains and emphasizes nutrient-dense foods and beverages—vegetables, fruits," etc.
- Ask for volunteers to help serve and distribute the foods you have selected for tasting.
- While people are eating, outline the benefits of eating plenty of fruits and veggies (vitamins, minerals, nutrients, fiber, etc). For more information, visit *www.choosemyplate.gov* and use the MyPlate handout included in this book.

Final question:
What vitamins and nutrients are in this dish? How will they affect your health?

Veggie Tart:

ChooseMyPlate.gov

Ingredients:
1 supermarket veggie platter or four cups of assorted chopped vegetables
1/4 cup ranch dressing
1 pint lowfat ricotta cheese
1/2 cup cooked spinach

Directions:
Put your the platter of veggies off to the side, then puree the remaining ingredients together in a food processor or with hand beaters. It may help to roughly chop the cooked spinach before incorporating it into the dip. Pour said dip into a tart pan and top with raw vegetables. Arrange the veggies in a circular pattern, and make sure the bottom of each is firmly anchored in the dip. Serve immediately or refrigerate for up to one hour until ready to serve.

Make It MyPlate:
This veggie dish is great for buffets so guests can fill 1/4 to half their plate.

Ingredient List:
Fresh, assorted chopped veggies like carrots, celery, tomatoes, cauliflower, broccoli, sugar snap peas, bell peppers, etc
Ranch dressing
Lowfat ricotta cheese
Cooked spinach (steamed fresh spinach or reheated frozen varieties are two great options)

Equipment List:
Measuring cups and spoons
Knife
Cutting board
Food processor or hand beaters and a bowl
Tart pan

Paper Goods and Misc:
Plates, napkins, and forks for tasting
Paper towels for kitchen cleanup
Baggies and plastic cups for prepped ingredients
Cleaning supplies for kitchen sanitation

Fun with Half the Plate

Handouts:
• MyPlate, MyPlate Shopping List

Label reading lesson:
• When selecting frozen or canned options, heed My-Plate's advice and compare the sodium content in a variety of brands, then choose the option with the lowest sodium. This also applies to added sugars.
• You can also avoid labels completely and shoot for fresh, whole fruits and veggies when possible.

Get Organized - To Do Lists:

What to do ahead of time:
• Copy all handouts.
• Measure and chop all ingredients and place them in plastic bags or cups.

Start class:
• Greet the class and distribute handouts.
• Ask how many are familiar with MyPlate's call to make half their plates full of fruits and veggies at each meal.

During class:
• Explain the importance of getting enough fruits and vegetables every day. Highlight these dishes as a great way to fill half your plate with fruits and vegetables.
• Repeat the advice from the Dietary Guidelines for Americans, "A healthy eating pattern limits intake of sodium, solid fats, added sugars, and refined grains and emphasizes nutrient-dense foods and beverages—vegetables, fruits," etc.
• Ask for volunteers to help serve and distribute the foods you have selected for tasting.
• While people are eating, outline the benefits of eating plenty of fruits and veggies (vitamins, minerals, nutrients, fiber, etc). For more information, visit *www.choosemyplate.gov* and use the MyPlate handout included in this book.

Final question:
What do you like to grill that is lean?

BBQ Sides:

ChooseMyPlate.gov

Ingredients:
Cubed, fresh fruit
Prepackaged coleslaw mix or fresh shredded cabbage
Bag of matchstick cut carrots
Light Ranch or Caesar dressing
Black sesame seeds (for garnish)
Flat leaf parsley (for garnish)

Directions:
Thread the cubed fresh fruit onto a bamboo skewer until the skewer is full. Repeat until you've used up all your fruit. Serve immediately or refrigerate until ready to serve.
Toss coleslaw mix and matchstick carrots together with the dressing until everything is lightly coated. Serve immediately or refrigerate until ready to serve. Garnish with black sesame seeds and flat leaf parsley, or shake on a bit of paprika.

Make It MyPlate:
• Lean BBQ protein sources like turkey burgers, veggie burgers, or grilled, marinated tofu.

Ingredient List:
Cubed fresh fruit like cantalope, honeydew, watermelon, pineapple, peaches, plums, or oranges
Prepackaged coleslaw mix or fresh shredded cabbage
Matchstick cut carrots
Light Ranch or Caesar salad dressing
Black sesame seeds
Flat leaf parsley

Equipment List:
Large bowl
Cutting board
Knife
Attractive dinner plate

Paper Goods and Misc:
Wooden skewers
Plates, napkins, and forks for tasting
Paper towels for kitchen cleanup
Baggies and plastic cups for ingredients
Cleaning supplies for kitchen sanitation

Fun with Half the Plate

Handouts:
• MyPlate, MyPlate Shopping List

Label reading lesson:
• When selecting frozen or canned options, heed My-Plate's advice and compare the sodium content in a variety of brands, then choose the option with the lowest sodium. This also applies to added sugars.
• You can also avoid labels completely and shoot for fresh, whole fruits and veggies when possible.

Get Organized - To Do Lists:

What to do ahead of time:
• Copy all handouts.
• Measure and chop all ingredients. Place them in plastic bags or cups.

Start class:
• Greet the class and distribute handouts.
• Ask how many are familiar with MyPlate's call to make half their plates full of fruits and veggies at each meal.

During class:
• Explain the importance of getting enough fruits and vegetables every day. Highlight this dish as a great way to fill part of your plate with veggies.
• Repeat the advice from the Dietary Guidelines for Americans, "A healthy eating pattern limits intake of sodium, solid fats, added sugars, and refined grains and emphasizes nutrient-dense foods and beverages—vegetables, fruits," etc.
• Ask for volunteers to help serve and distribute the foods you have selected for tasting.
• While people are eating, outline the benefits of eating plenty of fruits and veggies (vitamins, minerals, nutrients, fiber, etc). For more information, visit *www.choosemyplate.gov* and use the MyPlate handout included in this book.

Final question:
Which protein and fruit items would you serve with this delicious vegetable salad?

Eggplant Parmesan Salad:

Ingredients:
1 tablespoon extra virgin olive oil
2 tsp minced garlic
1 diced eggplant
3 diced tomatoes (use ripe red plum tomatoes)
2 tablespoons red wine vinegar
1 tsp Italian seasoning (dried basil, oregano, etc)
Watercress
Shaved fresh fennel
Squirt of balsamic glaze
Fresh cracked black pepper
Grated Parmesan cheese

Directions:
Heat the olive oil in a nonstick skillet. Saute the garlic until nutty, about 1-2 minutes. Add the eggplant and cook briefly then add the tomatoes and seasonings. Toss together then add the vinegar. Cover and allow the eggplant salad to cool briefly. (This can be done overnight in a fridge, if applicable).
Toss the water cress with a little bit of olive oil and arrange on a platter. Top with eggplant parmesan salad and Parmesan cheese. Garnish with shaved fresh fennel, a squirt of balsamic vinegar glaze and black pepper.

Ingredient List:
Extra virgin olive oil
Garlic
Eggplant
Tomatoes
Red wine vinegar
Italian seasoning
Watercress
Fennel
Balsamic glaze
Black pepper
Parmesan cheese

Equipment List:
Measuring cups and spoons
Knife
Cutting board
Stove top burner (can use a portable one)
Nonstick skillet
Cooking spoon
Grater
Serving spoon
Attractive platter

Paper Goods and Misc:
Plates, napkins and forks for tasting
Paper towels for kitchen cleanup
Baggies and plastic cups for ingredients
Cleaning supplies for kitchen sanitation

Veggie Tart:

Ingredients:
1 supermarket veggie platter or four
cups of assorted chopped vegetables
1/4 cup ranch dressing
1 pint lowfat ricotta cheese
1/2 cup cooked spinach

ChooseMyPlate.gov

Directions:
Put your the platter of veggies off to the side, then puree the remaining ingredients together in a food processor or with hand beaters. It may help to roughly chop the cooked spinach before incorporating it into the dip. Pour said dip into a tart pan and top with raw vegetables. Arrange the veggies in a circular pattern, and make sure the bottom of each is firmly anchored in the dip. Serve immediately or refrigerate for up to one hour until ready to serve.

Make It MyPlate:
• Whole grain crackers make a great addition to the tart. Just serve them in a basket on the side.

Ingredient List:	bowl
Fresh, assorted chopped veggies like carrots, celery, tomatoes, cauliflower, broccoli, sugar snap peas, bell peppers, etc	Tart pan
Ranch dressing	**Paper Goods and Misc:**
Lowfat ricotta cheese	Plates, napkins, and forks for tasting
Cooked spinach (steamed fresh spinach or reheated frozen varieties are two great options)	Paper towels for kitchen cleanup
	Baggies and plastic cups for prepped ingredients
Equipment List:	Cleaning supplies for kitchen sanitation
Measuring cups and spoons	
Knife	
Cutting board	
Food processor or hand beaters and a	

BBQ Sides:

Ingredients:
Cubed, fresh fruit
Prepackaged coleslaw mix or fresh shredded cabbage
Bag of matchstick cut carrots
Light Ranch or Caesar dressing
Black sesame seeds (for garnish)
Flat leaf parsley (for garnish)

ChooseMyPlate.gov

Directions:
Thread the cubed fresh fruit onto a bamboo skewer until the skewer is full. Repeat until you've used up all your fruit. Serve immediately or refrigerate until ready to serve.
Toss coleslaw mix and matchstick carrots together with the dressing until everything is lightly coated. Serve immediately or refrigerate until ready to serve. Garnish with black sesame seeds and flat leaf parsley, or shake on a bit of paprika.

Make It MyPlate:
• Lean BBQ protein sources like turkey burgers, veggie burgers, or grilled, marinated tofu.

Ingredient List:	**Equipment List:**
Cubed fresh fruit like cantalope, honeydew, watermelon, pineapple, peaches, plums, or oranges	Large bowl
	Cutting board
	Knife
	Attractive dinner plate
Prepackaged coleslaw mix or fresh shredded cabbage	**Paper Goods and Misc:**
Matchstick cut carrots	Wooden skewers
Light Ranch or Caesar salad dressing	Plates, napkins, and forks for tasting
Black sesame seeds	Paper towels for kitchen cleanup
Flat leaf parsley	Baggies and plastic cups for ingredients
	Cleaning supplies for kitchen sanitation

Eggplant Parmesan Salad:

Ingredients:
1 tablespoon extra virgin olive oil
2 tsp minced garlic
1 diced eggplant
3 diced tomatoes (use ripe red plum tomatoes)
2 tablespoons red wine vinegar
1 tsp Italian seasoning (dried basil, oregano, etc)
Watercress
Shaved fresh fennel
Squirt of balsamic glaze
Fresh cracked black pepper
Grated Parmesan cheese

Directions:
Heat the olive oil in a nonstick skillet. Saute the garlic until nutty, about 1-2 minutes. Add the eggplant and cook briefly then add the tomatoes and seasonings. Toss together then add the vinegar. Cover and allow the eggplant salad to cool briefly. (This can be done overnight in a fridge, if applicable).

Toss the water cress with a little bit of olive oil and arrange on a platter. Top with eggplant parmesan salad and Parmesan cheese. Garnish with shaved fresh fennel, a squirt of balsamic vinegar glaze and black pepper.

Make It MyPlate:
Serve with a whole grain, a lean protein item and a side of fruit.

Ingredient List:	Equipment List:
Extra virgin olive oil	Measuring cups and
Garlic	spoons
Eggplant	Knife
Tomatoes	Cutting board
Red wine vinegar	
Italian seasoning	
Watercress	
Fennel	
Balsamic glaze	
Black pepper	
Parmesan cheese	

Salad Lesson

Handouts:
• MyPlate, MyPlate Shopping List, Recipe

Get Organized - To Do Lists:

What to do ahead of time:
• Copy all handouts.
• Measure and chop all ingredients. Place them in plastic bags or cups.

Start class:
• Ask who has ever made a salad as an entree for dinner? Explain that we are going to prepare a light salad that comes together in minutes - and pairs nicely with soup and bread/crackers.
• Distribute handouts.

During class:
• Have a volunteer come and help you assemble the salad.
• Put each item into the bowl, explaining what it is and how you prepared it. Talk about the importance of getting enough vegetables.
• Toss the salad, then place part of it on a large dinner plate so the group can see how it should be presented. Garnish with whole grain bread or crackers.
• You might want to make all of the salads in this section or pair this with another dish in the My-Plate demo kit.
• Ask for a volunteer to help pass out tastings (volunteers need to wash their hands before starting).

Final question:
How many food groups did we use today? Which vegetable subgroups played a role?

Tuna Tomato Salad

Ingredients:
1 bag romaine lettuce
1 cup cherry tomatoes, halved
1/4 cup thinly sliced dried tomato
1/4 cup thinly sliced red onion
1/2 cup shredded carrots
1/2 cup thinly sliced bell pepper
1 can low-sodium tuna
1 Tbsp olive oil
juice of 1 lemon
Black pepper to taste

Directions: Toss all ingredients together in large salad bowl. Serve on chilled plates.

Make It MyPlate:
Serve with whole grain crackers and a side of fruit.

Ingredient List:
Romaine lettuce (bag)
1 box cherry tomatoes
1 bag dried tomato
1 red onion
1 carrot
1 green bell pepper
1 can low-sodium tuna
olive oil
1 lemon
Black pepper

Equipment List:
Measuring cups and spoons
Knife
Cutting board
Large salad bowl
Salad utensils
Attractive dinner plate

Paper Goods and Misc:
Plates, napkins, and forks for tasting
Paper towels for kitchen cleanup
Baggies and plastic cups for ingredients
Cleaning supplies for kitchen sanitation

Salad Lesson

Handouts:
• MyPlate, MyPlate Shopping List, Recipe

Get Organized - To Do Lists:

What to do ahead of time:
• Copy all handouts.
• Measure and chop all ingredients. Place them in plastic bags or cups.

Start class:
• Ask who has ever made a salad as an entree for dinner? Explain that we are going to prepare a light salad that comes together in minutes - and pairs nicely with grilled chicken or fish.
• Distribute handouts.

During class:
• Have a volunteer come and help you assemble the salad.
• Put each item into the bowl, explaining what it is and how you prepared it. Talk about the importance of getting enough vegetables.
• Toss the salad, then place part of it on a large dinner plate so the group can see how it should be presented. Garnish with whole grain bread or crackers.
• You might want to make all of the salads in this section or pair this with another dish in the MyPlate demo kit.
• Ask for a volunteer to help pass out tastings (volunteers need to wash their hands before starting).

Final question:
How many food groups did we use today? Which vegetable subgroups played a role?

Taco Salad

Ingredients:
1 bag romaine lettuce
14 oz can black beans, drained
1 cup diced tomato
1/2 cup diced green onion
1 tablespoon chopped cilantro or parsley
juice of 1 lime
1 cup crunched tortilla chips
Dash hot pepper sauce

Directions: Toss ingredients in large salad bowl. Serve immediately. If making ahead, do not put lime juice, tortilla chips or hot pepper until the last minute.

Make It MyPlate:
Add a side of fruit and more grains if you like - we suggest brown rice or a whole grain corn tortill.

Ingredient List:
1 bag romaine lettuce
1 can black beans
1 tomato
1 bunch green onion
cilantro or parsley
lime
tortilla chips (can use snack size bag)
hot pepper sauce

If you want you can add a piece of grilled chicken or fish.

Equipment List:
Measuring cups and spoons
Knife
Cutting board
Large bowl
Salad utensils
Serving spoon
Attractive dinner plate

Paper Goods and Misc:
Plates, napkins, and forks for tasting
Paper towels for kitchen cleanup
Baggies and plastic cups for ingredients
Cleaning supplies for kitchen sanitation

Salad Lesson

Handouts:
• MyPlate, MyPlate Shopping List, Recipe

Label reading lesson:

Get Organized - To Do Lists:

What to do ahead of time:
• Copy all handouts.
• Measure and chop all ingredients. Place them in plastic bags or cups.

Start class:
• Ask who has ever made a salad as an entree for dinner? Explain that we are going to prepare a dinner salad that comes together in minutes. It's an entree and a salad in one!
• Distribute handouts.

During class:
• Have a volunteer come and help you assemble the meal.
• Put each item into the bowl, explaining what it is and how you prepared it. Talk about the importance of getting enough vegetables.
• Toss the salad, then place part of it on a large dinner plate so the group can see how it should be presented. Garnish with whole grain bread or crackers.
• You might want to make all of the salads in this section or pair this with another dish in the MyPlate demo kit.
• Ask for a volunteer to help pass out tastings (volunteers need to wash their hands before starting).

Final question:
How many food groups did we use today? Which vegetable subgroups played a role?

Chicken Rice Salad

Ingredients:
1 bag romaine lettuce
1 cup cooked skinless chicken breast, chop
2 cups cooked brown rice
1 cup chopped red bell pepper
1 cup diced tomato
1/2 cup diced red onion
Juice of one lemon
1/2 tsp oregano
Pinch cumin
Pinch chili powder
Pinch coriander
Black pepper to taste
Pinch garlic powder
Directions: cook the rice and chill; assemble salad by tossing all ingredients together in a large bowl. Serve immediately. If you want to make ahead, add lemon juice and toss at the last minute.

Make It MyPlate:
Corn bread and fresh fruit.

Ingredient List:
romaine lettuce
cooked chicken breast
minute brown rice
red pepper
tomato
red onion
lemon
oregani
cumin
chili powder
coriander
black pepper
garlic powder

cornbread for garnish
(optional)

Equipment List:
Measuring cups and spoons

Knife
Cutting board
Stove top burner (can use portable one)
Small pan
Large bowl
Salad utensils
Cooking spoon
Attractive dinner plate

Paper Goods and Misc:
Plates, napkins, and forks for tasting
Paper towels for kitchen cleanup
Baggies and plastic cups for ingredients
Cleaning supplies for kitchen sanitation

Tuna Tomato Salad

Ingredients:
1 bag romaine lettuce
1 cup cherry tomatoes, halved
1/4 cup thinly sliced dried tomato
1/4 cup thinly sliced red onion
1/2 cup shredded carrots
1/2 cup thinly sliced bell pepper
1 can low-sodium tuna
1 Tbsp olive oil
juice of 1 lemon
Black pepper to taste

Directions: Toss all ingredients together in large salad bowl. Serve on chilled plates.

Make It MyPlate:

Add whole grain crackers and a side of fruit.

Ingredient List:	Equipment List:
Romaine lettuce (bag)	Measuring cups and spoons
1 box cherry tomatoes	Knife
1 bag dried tomato	Cutting board
1 red onion	Large salad bowl
1 carrot	Salad utensils
1 green bell pepper	Attractive dinner plate
1 can low-sodium tuna	
olive oil	**Paper Goods and Misc:**
1 lemon	Plates, napkins, and forks for tasting
Black pepper	Paper towels for kitchen cleanup
	Baggies and plastic cups for ingredients
	Cleaning supplies for kitchen sanitation

Taco Salad

Ingredients:
1 bag romaine lettuce
14 oz can black beans, drained
1 cup diced tomato
1/2 cup diced green onion
1 tablespoon chopped cilantro or parsley
juice of 1 lime
1 cup crunched tortilla chips
Dash hot pepper sauce

Directions: Toss ingredients in large salad bowl. Serve immediately. If making ahead, do not put lime juice, tortilla chips or hot pepper until the last minute.

Make It MyPlate:

Add more whole grains like brown rice or a whole grain corn tortilla and a side of fruit.

Ingredient List:	Equipment List:
1 bag romaine lettuce	Measuring cups and spoons
1 can black beans	Knife
1 tomato	Cutting board
1 bunch green onion	Large bowl
cilantro or parsley	Salad utensils
lime	Serving spoon
tortilla chips (can use snack size bag)	Attractive dinner plate
hot pepper sauce	
	Paper Goods and Misc:
If you want you can add a piece of grilled chicken or fish.	Plates, napkins, and forks for tasting
	Paper towels for kitchen cleanup
	Baggies and plastic cups for ingredients
	Cleaning supplies for kitchen sanitation

Chicken Rice Salad

Ingredients:
1 bag romaine lettuce
1 cup cooked skinless chicken breast, chop
2 cups cooked brown rice
1 cup chopped red bell pepper
1 cup diced tomato
1/2 cup diced red onion
Juice of one lemon
1/2 tsp oregano
Pinch cumin
Pinch chili powder
Pinch coriander
Black pepper to taste
Pinch garlic powder

Directions: cook the rice and chill; assemble salad by tossing all ingredients together in a large bowl. Serve immediately. If you want to make ahead, add lemon juice and toss at the last minute.

Make It MyPlate:
Add a side of fruit.

Ingredient List:	Equipment List:
romaine lettuce	Measuring cups and spoons
cooked chicken breast	Knife
minute brown rice	Cutting board
red pepper	Stove top burner (can use portable one)
tomato	Small pan
red onion	Large bowl
lemon	Salad utensils
oregani	Cooking spoon
cumin	Attractive dinner plate
chili powder	
coriander	**Paper Goods and Misc:**
black pepper	Plates, napkins, and forks for tasting
garlic powder	Paper towels for kitchen cleanup
cornbread for garnish (optional)	Baggies and plastic cups for ingredients

Healthy Assembly Meals

Handouts:
• MyPlate, MyPlate Shopping List, Recipe

Label reading lesson:
• Compare the fat and sodium in similar burritos from Taco Bell (or other Mexican restaurants). Explain that this option is lower in fat and sodium.

Get Organized - To Do Lists:

What to do ahead of time:
• Copy all handouts.
• Measure and chop all ingredients. Place them in plastic bags or cups.

Start class:
• Greet the class and distribute handouts.
• Ask who would like to make dinner in 15 minutes or less?
• Ask how long it takes to drive to a restaurant and pick up takeout for dinner, then drive home. The dinner we are going to make today takes less time and does not require any complicated preparation

During class:
• Have all ingredients lined up and ready to go. Have someone in the audience time you to see how long it takes to roll 4 burritos.
• Cut the burritos and pass out samples for tastings. It is fun if you can make a buffet and allow people to make their own burritos too.

Final question:
How many food groups did we use today? How many servings from each one?

---

15 Minute Burritos

Ingredients:
4 medium flour tortillas
1 can beans, drained and re-heated
2 cups cooked brown rice (use minute rice)
1/4 cup salsa
1/2 cup fat-free sour cream

Heat beans and rice. Warm the tortillas in the microwave for 20 seconds each. Divide the ingredients between the tortillas and roll up. Serve hot. They can be reheated in the microwave if necessary.

Make It MyPlate:
Add more veggies and fruit.

Ingredient List:
flour tortillas
canned pinto beans
minute brown rice
prepared salsa
fat-free sourcream

Optional: ingredients to make a large salad.

Equipment List:
Measuring cups and spoons
Knife
Cutting board
Microwave
Microwave containers
Serving spoon
Attractive dinner plate

Paper Goods and Misc:
Plates, napkins, and forks for tasting
Paper towels for kitchen cleanup
Baggies and plastic cups for ingredients
Cleaning supplies for kitchen sanitation

© Food & Health Communications *www.foodandhealth.com*

Healthy Assembly Meals

Handouts:
• MyPlate, MyPlate Shopping List, Recipe

Label reading lesson:
• Compare the fat and sodium in similar foods from Taco Bell (or other Mexican restaurants). Explain that this option is lower in fat and sodium.

Get Organized - To Do Lists:

What to do ahead of time:
• Copy all handouts.
• Measure and chop all ingredients. Place them in plastic bags or cups.

Start class:
• Greet the class and distribute handouts.
• Ask who would like to make dinner in 15 minutes or less?
• Ask how long it takes to drive to a restaurant and pick up takeout for dinner, then drive home. The dinner we are going to make today takes less time and does not require any complicated preparation

During class:
• Have all ingredients lined up and ready to go. Have someone in the audience time you to see how long it takes to make 4 tostada salads.
• Make mini salads for tastings or make a buffet and let everyone make their own.

Final question:
How many food groups did we use today? How many servings from each one?

Tostada Salad

Ingredients:
4 medium corn tortillas
1 bag ready-to-serve romaine lettuce
1 cup cherry tomatoes
1 can beans, drained and re-heated
4 Tbsp red wine vinegar
1/4 cup salsa
1/2 cup fat-free sour cream
Heat beans. Toast the corn tortillas in the oven for about 10 minutes or until lightly golden. Place the toasted tortillas on a plate and top with lettuce, tomatoes, warmed beans, vinegar, salsa and sour cream. Serve immediately. For fun and more flavor you can add diced mango and fresh lime.

Make It MyPlate:
Add some fruit.

Ingredient List:
corn tortillas
bag romaine lettuce
box cherry tomatoes
vinegar
canned pinto beans
prepared salsa
fat-free sourcream

Optional: grilled chicken or fish, side of minute brown rice, mango and lime (to add fruit)

Equipment List:
Measuring cups and spoons
Knife
Cutting board
Microwave
Microwave containers
Serving spoon
Attractive dinner plate

Paper Goods and Misc:
Plates, napkins, and forks for tasting
Paper towels for kitchen cleanup
Baggies and plastic cups for ingredients
Cleaning supplies for kitchen sanitation

Healthy Assembly Meals

Handouts:
- MyPlate, MyPlate Shopping List, Recipe

Label reading lesson:
- Compare the fat and sodium from online pizza places (check out their websites for nutrition facts) or from frozen pizzas. How do they measure up to this version?

Get Organized - To Do Lists:

What to do ahead of time:
- Copy all handouts.
- Measure and chop all ingredients. Place them in plastic bags or cups.

Start class:
- Greet the class and distribute handouts.
- Ask who would like to make dinner in 15 minutes or less?
- Ask how long it takes to drive to a restaurant and pick up takeout for dinner, then drive home. The dinner we are going to make today takes less time and does not require any complicated preparation

During class:
- Have all ingredients lined up and ready to go. Have someone in the audience time you to see how long it takes to make 4 pizzas. It is fun if you can make 4 different varieties: cheese, onion, mushroom, very veggie, pineapple/pepper, etc. It could also be fun to ask for volunteers and audience creations!
- Distribute tasting samples or set up a pizza buffet and allow the group to choose their pizza slices.

Final question:
How many food groups did we use today? How many servings from each one? Which lean protein item and fruit would go great with this dish?

Tortilla Pizza

Ingredients:
4 medium flour tortillas
8 tablespoons pasta sauce
2 cups sliced fresh veggies (assorted)
1/2 cup light mozzarella cheese or 4 tablespoons parmesan cheese

Preheat oven to 350 degrees or use toaster oven. Place tortillas on baking pan. Spread each one with 2 tablespoons pasta sauce. Top each one with sliced veggies and shredded cheese. Bake in the oven untl the tortillas are golden and the cheese is melted and the vegetables are heated through, about 10-12 minutes. Serve hot.

Make It MyPlate:
This counts as a grain and vegetable. You should add a lean protein item and fresh fruit.

Ingredient List:
flour torillas
pasta sauce
mozzarella cheese
assorted fresh veggies: onions, broccoli, zucchini, mushrooms

Optional: Ingredients for large tossed salad.

Equipment List:
Measuring cups and spoons
Knife
Cutting board
Microwave
Microwave containers
Serving spoon
Attractive dinner plate

Paper Goods and Misc:
Plates, napkins, and forks for tasting
Paper towels for kitchen cleanup
Baggies and plastic cups for ingredients
Cleaning supplies for kitchen sanitation

Healthy Assembly Meals

Handouts:
• MyPlate, MyPlate Shopping List, Recipe

Label reading lesson:
• Compare the fat and sodium in frozen lasagna to this creation.

Get Organized - To Do Lists:

What to do ahead of time:
• Copy all handouts.
• Make and bake on lasagna. Have ingredients ready to show how to assemble another.

Start class:
• Greet the class and distribute handouts.
• Ask who would like to make dinner in 15 minutes or less?
• Ask how long it takes to drive to a restaurant and pick up takeout for dinner, then drive home. The dinner we are going to make today takes less time and does not require any complicated preparation. This takes about 5 minutes to assemble and 1 hour of unattended time to bake.

During class:
• Have all ingredients lined up and ready to go. Have someone in the audience time you to see how long it takes to prepare 1 pan of lasagna.
• Slice the cooked lasagna into small pieces for tastings.

Final question:
How many food groups did we use today? How many servings from each one?

Lasagna

Ingredients:
1 box no boil lasagna noodles
1.5 jars pasta sauce (26 oz)
1 quart tub fat-free ricotta cheese
1 cup light shredded mozzarella cheese

Preheat oven to 350 degrees. Layer noodles, sauce and ricotta until they are used up in a large 9X12 baking dish or pan. Cover with sauce and then mozzarella on top. Cover with foil and bake one hour or until noodles are tender. Cool slightly then cut into 8 squares. Serve hot.

Make It MyPlate:

Lasagna is grains and veggies so it can take up half the plate and count for dairy, too. Add a bit of lean protein and fruit for the other half of the plate.

Ingredient List:
no-boil lasagna noodles
2 jars pasta sauce
1 bag light mozzsarella
1 quart fat-free ricotta cheese

Optional: Ingredients for large tossed salad.

Equipment List:
Measuring cups and spoons
spatula
Oven
9X12 baking dish
Knife
Serving spoon
Attractive dinner plate

Paper Goods and Misc:

Plates, napkins, and forks for tasting
Paper towels for kitchen cleanup
Baggies and plastic cups for ingredients
Cleaning supplies for kitchen sanitation

Healthy Assembly Meals

Handouts:
• MyPlate, MyPlate Shopping List, Recipe

Label reading lesson:
• Compare the fat and sodium from a tuna sandwich from a restaurant to the tuna sandwich here. If you need it, Panera Bread has nutritional information online.

Get Organized - To Do Lists:

What to do ahead of time:
• Copy all handouts.
• Have ingredients ready.

Start class:
• Greet the class and distribute handouts.
• Ask who likes to prepare dinner in 15 minutes or less?
• Ask how long it takes to drive to get takeout for dinner and then drive home. This dinner takes less time and does not require any complicated preparation. It takes about 5 minutes to assemble.

During class:
• Have all ingredients lined up and ready to go. Have someone in the audience time you to see how long it takes to make the sandwiches.
• Slice sandwiches into smaller pieces for tastings.

Final question:
How many food groups did we use today? How many servings from each one? Which fruit would you use?

Open-Faced Tuna Sandwich

Ingredients:
1 can low-sodium tuna
3 tablespoons light mayonnaise
4 pieces whole grain toast
1 large tomato, sliced
1 bag romaine lettuce (ready to serve)
1 bag baby carrots
1 stalk green onion

Mash tuna and mayo in small bowl. Toast bread. Top bread with lettuce, tuna and sliced tomato. Garnish with sliced green onion. Serve baby carrots on the side. Makes 4 open faced sandwiches.

Make It MyPlate:
This recipe uses fish, whole grain toast and veggies. Add some apple slices or other fruit.

Ingredient List:
1 can low-sodium tuna
1 jar light mayo
1 large ripe tomato
1 bag romaine lettuce
1 stalk green onion
1 bag baby carrots
4 slices whole grain bread

Optional: Lowfat soup to serve with sandwich.

Equipment List:
Can opener
fork
small bowl
knife
cutting board
1 serving plate

Paper Goods and Misc:
Plates, napkins, and forks for tasting
Paper towels for kitchen cleanup
Baggies and plastic cups for ingredients
Cleaning supplies for kitchen sanitation

Healthy Assembly Meals

Handouts:
• MyPlate, MyPlate Shopping List, Recipe

Label reading lesson:
• Compare fat-free sour cream to regular sour cream. How does saturated fat content differ? How about taste?

Get Organized - To Do Lists:

What to do ahead of time:
• Copy all handouts.
• Measure and chop all ingredients. Place them in plastic bags or cups.
• Start cooking potatoes before class begins.

Start class:
• Greet the class and distribute handouts.
• Ask how many have ever made a meal out of a baked potato.

During class:
• Explain the nutritional importance of a potato. Outline the vitamins and minerals that it contains, and discuss its (undeserved) bad reputation. How does frying affect the nutritional profile of foods?
• Ask for volunteers to help serve and distribute the potato (and salad... if you make it).

Final question:
This is a delicious vegetable dish that goes on 1/4th of the plate. Let's figure out what else we can add to make it a meal.

Stuffed Baked Potato

Ingredients:
4 medium baking potatoes
8 tablespoons fat-free sour cream
black pepper to taste
4 cups broccoli florets, rinsed
2 tablespoons grated Parmesan cheese

Directions:
Wash potatoes and pierce with a fork. Bake for 3 minutes per potato in the microwave - turn over and bake again until done, usually about one more minute per potato. Steam broccoli or microwave in covered container. Cut each potato in half lengthwise and place on plate. Fluff inside with a fork. Divide sour cream between potatoes and season with black pepper. Place 1 cup of steamed broccoli inside each potato. Sprinkle with 1/2 tablespoon Parmesan cheese per potato.

Make It MyPlate:
Add a lean protein item, whole grain and fruit.

Ingredient List:
4 baking potatoes
fat-free sour cream
black pepper
4 cups broccoli florets
Parmesan cheese (grated)

Optional: make a large tossed salad to go with the potato. Have regular sourcream to show label reading lesson - compare the two.

Equipment List:
Measuring cups and spoons
Knife
Cutting board
Microwave
Fork
Serving spoon
Attractive dinner plate

Paper Goods and Misc:
Plates, napkins, and forks for tasting
Paper towels for kitchen cleanup
Baggies and plastic cups for ingredients
Cleaning supplies for kitchen sanitation

Healthy Assembly Meals

Handouts:
• MyPlate, MyPlate Shopping List, Recipe

Label reading lesson:
• Compare sodium in pita pockets to regular bread or rolls - pita pockets are usually low in sodium and high in fiber
• Compare sodium found in various Italian dressings

Get Organized - To Do Lists:

What to do ahead of time:
• Copy all handouts.
• Measure and chop all ingredients. Place them in plastic bags or cups.
• If you really wan tthis recipe to go fast, cook the chicken tenders ahead of time.

Start class:
• Greet the class and distribute handouts.
• Ask how many make sandwiches for dinner?

During class:
• Ask for volunteers to help assemble and pass out tastes of the Greek Chicken Pita Pockets.
• Make the pita pockets by following the directions.
• Show how attractive they can be when arranged on dinner plate together.

Final question:
How many food groups did we use today? How many servings from each one?

Greek Chicken Pita Pocket

Ingredients:
8 ounces skinless chicken tenders
1/4 cup low-fat Italian dressing
4 whole wheat pita pockets, warmed
4 cups romaine lettuce
1/2 cup cherry tomatoes, halved
Sliced red onion - sliced in thin rings

Directions:
Place chicken tenders in microwave in level dish (do not stack tenders). Microwave on chicken setting or on high power until chicken is done, about 5 minutes. Make sure chicken is not pink in the middle. Cut the pita pockets in half. Divide the lettuce, chicken, tomatoes and dressing between the pockets. Garnish each with a red onion ring. Serve immediately.

Make It MyPlate:
Add a nice seasonal fruit salad.

Ingredient List:	Equipment List:
8 oz chicken tenders	Measuring cups and
Italian dressing	spoons
Whole wheat pita pockets	Knife
Bag romaine lettuce	Cutting board
Cherry tomatoes	Microwave oven
Red onion	Microwave container
	Cooking spoon
	Serving spoon
Optional: Lowfat soup	Attractive dinner plate

Paper Goods and Misc:
Plates, napkins, and forks for tasting
Paper towels for kitchen cleanup
Baggies and plastic cups for ingredients
Cleaning supplies for kitchen sanitation

Healthy Assembly Meals

Handouts:
• MyPlate, MyPlate Shopping List, Recipe

Label reading lesson:
• Compare sodium in canned chili and in tomatoes that are made with salt and without salt.

Get Organized - To Do Lists:

What to do ahead of time:
• Copy all handouts.
• Measure and chop all ingredients. Place them in plastic bags or cups.
• If you really want preparation of this recipe to go quickly, start cooking the chili in the microwave ahead of time.

Start class:
• Greet the class and distribute handouts.
• Ask how many get beans in their diet each week?

During class:
• Ask for volunteers to help assemble the chili.
• Show the audience how to chop onions and peppers and discuss frozen versions for those who don't like to cook.
• Finish preparing chili, then distribute taste samples to the group.

Final question:
How many food groups did we use today? How many servings from each one?

Microwave Chili

ChooseMyPlate.gov

Ingredients:
4 ounces lean ground turkey or beef
1/2 cup chopped onions*
1/4 cup chopped green peppers*
14 ounce can pinto beans, and liquid
14 ounce can cut up peeled whole tomatoes with juice
1 teaspoon garlic powder
2 tablespoons chili powder
1/2 teaspoon cumin
6 ounce can tomato paste
*can use frozen

Directions:
Place all ingredients in large microwaveable casserole dish. Cover; and place in microwave on full power for 20 minutes. Stir every 5 or 10 minutes.

Make It MyPlate:
Add brown rice and a side of fruit.

Ingredient List:	Equipment List:
lean ground turkey or beef	Measuring cups and spoons
onion	Can opener
green pepper	Knife
pinto beans	Cutting board
canned tomatoes	Microwave
garlic powder	Microwave container
chili powder	Cooking spoon
cumin	Serving spoon
tomato paste	Attractive dinner plate

Ingredient (continued): Optional: Canned chili mixes for comparison. Also - canned tomatoes with salt and canned tomatoes without salt so they can see the difference.

Paper Goods and Misc:
Plates, napkins, and forks for tasting
Paper towels for kitchen cleanup
Baggies and plastic cups for ingredients
Cleaning supplies for kitchen sanitation

15 Minute Burritos

Ingredients:
4 medium flour tortillas
1 can beans, drained and re-heated
2 cups cooked brown rice (use minute rice)
1/4 cup salsa
1/2 cup fat-free sour cream

Heat beans and rice. Warm the tortillas in the microwave for 20 seconds each. Divide the ingredients between the tortillas and roll up. Serve hot. They can be reheated in the microwave if necessary.

Make It MyPlate:
Fresh fruit.

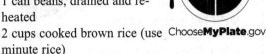
ChooseMyPlate.gov

Ingredient List:	**Equipment List:**
flour torillas	Measuring cups and
canned pinto beans	spoons
minute brown rice	Knife
prepared salsa	Cutting board
fat-free sourcream	Microwave
	Microwave containers
Optional: ingredients to	Serving spoon
make a large salad.	Attractive dinner plate

Paper Goods and Misc:
Plates, napkins, and forks for tasting
Paper towels for kitchen cleanup
Baggies and plastic cups for ingredients
Cleaning supplies for kitchen sanitation

Tostada Salad

Ingredients:
4 medium corn tortillas
1 bag ready-to-serve romaine lettuce
1 cup cherry tomatoes
1 can beans, drained and re-heated
4 Tbsp red wine vinegar
1/4 cup salsa
1/2 cup fat-free sour cream

Heat beans. Toast the corn tortillas in the oven for about 10 minutes or until lightly golden. Place the toasted tortillas on a plate and top with lettuce, tomatoes, warmed beans, vinegar, salsa and sour cream. Serve immediately. For fun and more flavor you can add diced mango and fresh lime.

Make It MyPlate:
Fresh fruit.

ChooseMyPlate.gov

Ingredient List:	**Equipment List:**
corn torillas	Measuring cups and
bag romaine lettuce	spoons
box cherry tomatoes	Knife
vinegar	Cutting board
canned pinto beans	Microwave
prepared salsa	Microwave containers
fat-free sourcream	Serving spoon
	Attractive dinner plate
Optional: grilled chicken or fish, side of minute brown rice, mango and lime (to add fruit)	

Paper Goods and Misc:
Plates, napkins, and forks for tasting
Paper towels for kitchen cleanup
Baggies and plastic cups for ingredients
Cleaning supplies for kitchen sanitation

Tortilla Pizza

Ingredients:
4 medium flour tortillas
8 tablespoons pasta sauce
2 cups sliced fresh veggies (assorted)
1/2 cup light mozzarella cheese or 4 tablespoons parmesan cheese

Preheat oven to 350 degrees or use toaster oven. Place tortillas on baking pan. Spread each one with 2 tablespoons pasta sauce. Top each one with sliced veggies and shredded cheese. Bake in the oven untl the tortillas are golden and the cheese is melted and the vegetables are heated through, about 10-12 minutes. Serve hot.

Make It MyPlate:
Lean protein and fruit.

Ingredient List:	Equipment List:
flour tortillas	Measuring cups and spoons
pasta sauce	Knife
mozzarella cheese	Cutting board
assorted fresh veggies: onions, broccoli, zucchini, mushrooms	Microwave
	Microwave containers
	Serving spoon
Optional: Ingredients for large tossed salad.	Attractive dinner plate

Paper Goods and Misc:
Plates, napkins, and forks for tasting
Paper towels for kitchen cleanup
Baggies and plastic cups for ingredients
Cleaning supplies for kitchen sanitation

Lasagna

Ingredients:
1 box no boil lasagna noodles
1.5 jars pasta sauce (26 oz)
1 quart tub fat-free ricotta cheese
1 cup light shredded mozzarella cheese

Preheat oven to 350 degrees. Layer noodles, sauce and ricotta until they are used up in a large 9X12 baking dish or pan. Cover with sauce and then mozzarella on top. Cover with foil and bake one hour or until noodles are tender. Cool slightly then cut into 8 squares. Serve hot.

Make It MyPlate:
Lean protein and fruit.

Ingredient List:	Equipment List:
no-boil lasagna noodles	Measuring cups and spoons
2 jars pasta sauce	spatula
1 bag light mozzsarella	Oven
1 quart fat-free ricotta cheese	9X12 baking dish
	Knife
	Serving spoon
Optional: Ingredients for large tossed salad.	Attractive dinner plate

Paper Goods and Misc:
Plates, napkins, and forks for tasting
Paper towels for kitchen cleanup
Baggies and plastic cups for ingredients
Cleaning supplies for kitchen sanitation

Open-Faced Tuna Sandwich

ChooseMyPlate.gov

Ingredients:
1 can low-sodium tuna
3 tablespoons light mayonnaise
4 pieces whole grain toast
1 large tomato, sliced
1 bag romaine lettuce (ready to serve)
1 bag baby carrots
1 stalk green onion

Mash tuna and mayo in small bowl. Toast bread. Top bread with lettuce, tuna and sliced tomato. Garnish with sliced green onion. Serve baby carrots on the side. Makes 4 open faced sandwiches.

Make It MyPlate:
Side of fruit.

Ingredient List:	Equipment List:
1 can low-sodium tuna	Can opener
1 jar light mayo	fork
1 large ripe tomato	small bowl
1 bag romaine lettuce	knife
1 stalk green onion	cutting board
1 bag baby carrots	1 serving plate
4 slices whole grain bread	
	Paper Goods and Misc:
Optional: Lowfat soup to serve with sandwich.	Plates, napkins, and forks for tasting
	Paper towels for kitchen cleanup
	Baggies and plastic cups for ingredients
	Cleaning supplies for kitchen sanitation

Stuffed Baked Potato

ChooseMyPlate.gov

Ingredients:
4 medium baking potatoes
8 tablespoons fat-free sour cream
black pepper to taste
4 cups broccoli florets, rinsed
2 tablespoons grated Parmesan cheese

Directions:
Wash potatoes and pierce with a fork. Bake for 3 minutes per potato in the microwave - turn over and bake again until done, usually about one more minute per potato. Steam broccoli or microwave in covered container. Cut each potato in half lengthwise and place on plate. Fluff inside with a fork. Divide sour cream between potatoes and season with black pepper. Place 1 cup of steamed broccoli inside each potato. Sprinkle with 1/2 tablespoon Parmesan cheese per potato.

Make It MyPlate:
Whole grain, lean protein, fruit.

Ingredient List:	Equipment List:
4 baking potatoes	Measuring cups and spoons
fat-free sour cream	Knife
black pepper	Cutting board
4 cups broccoli florets	Microwave
Parmesan cheese (grated)	Fork
	Serving spoon
Optional: make a large tossed salad to go with the potato. Have regular sourcream to show label reading lesson - compare the two.	Attractive dinner plate
	Paper Goods and Misc:
	Plates, napkins, and forks for tasting
	Paper towels for kitchen cleanup
	Baggies and plastic cups for ingredients
	Cleaning supplies for kitchen sanitation

Greek Chicken Pita Pocket

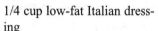
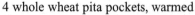

ChooseMyPlate.gov

Ingredients:
8 ounces skinless chicken tenders
1/4 cup low-fat Italian dressing
4 whole wheat pita pockets, warmed
4 cups romaine lettuce
1/2 cup cherry tomatoes, halved
Sliced red onion - sliced in thin rings

Directions:
Place chicken tenders in microwave in level dish (do not stack tenders). Microwave on chicken setting or on high power until chicken is done, about 5 minutes. Make sure chicken is not pink in the middle. Cut the pita pockets in half. Divide the lettuce, chicken, tomatoes and dressing between the pockets. Garnish each with a red onion ring. Serve immediately.

Make It MyPlate:
Fresh fruit.

Ingredient List:	Equipment List:
8 oz chicken tenders	Measuring cups and spoons
Italian dressing	Knife
Whole wheat pita pockets	Cutting board
Bag romaine lettuce	Microwave oven
Cherry tomatoes	Microwave container
Red onion	Cooking spoon
	Serving spoon
Optional: Lowfat soup	Attractive dinner plate

Paper Goods and Misc:
Plates, napkins, and forks for tasting
Paper towels for kitchen cleanup
Baggies and plastic cups for ingredients
Cleaning supplies for kitchen sanitation

Microwave Chili

ChooseMyPlate.gov

Ingredients:
4 ounces lean ground turkey or beef
1/2 cup chopped onions*
1/4 cup chopped green peppers*
14 ounce can pinto beans, and liquid
14 ounce can cut up peeled whole tomatoes with juice
1 teaspoon garlic powder
2 tablespoons chili powder
1/2 teaspoon cumin
6 ounce can tomato paste
*can use frozen

Directions:
Place all ingredients in large microwaveable casserole dish. Cover; and place in microwave on full power for 20 minutes. Stir every 5 or 10 minutes.

Make It MyPlate:
Brown rice or whole grain pasta, fresh fruit.

Ingredient List:	Equipment List:
lean ground turkey or beef	Measuring cups and spoons
onion	Can opener
green pepper	Knife
pinto beans	Cutting board
canned tomatoes	Microwave
garlic powder	Microwave container
chili powder	Cooking spoon
cumin	Serving spoon
tomato paste	Attractive dinner plate
Optional: Canned chili mixes for comparison. Also - canned tomatoes with salt and canned tomatoes without salt so they can see the difference.	**Paper Goods and Misc:** Plates, napkins, and forks for tasting Paper towels for kitchen cleanup Baggies and plastic cups for ingredients Cleaning supplies for

© Food & Health Communications *www.foodandhealth.com*

Breakfast Lesson

Handouts:
• MyPlate, MyPlate Shopping List, Breakfast, Recipe

Label reading lesson:
• Compare boxed cereal mixes and instant oatmeal packs to plain oatmeal. Draw attention to fiber and sodium content.
• Compare oatmeal to pastries from Dunkin' Donuts and McDonalds. Discuss the huge differences in calories and fat. Remind the group that most large muffins, Danish, bagels, and breakfast pastries contain more than 400 calories apiece.

Get Organized - To Do Lists:

What to do ahead of time:
• Copy all handouts.
• Make printouts of some of the nutrition facts for breakfast foods from popular restaurant websites. We recommend McDonalds.com, Starbucks.com and DunkinDonuts.com.
• Measure all ingredients and place them in plastic bags or cups.

Start class:
• Greet the class and distribute handouts.
• Ask how many eat breakfast in the morning.

During class:
• While the oatmeal is cooking, explain to the class the differences in types of oatmeal. Regular or minute is fine - and so is instant as long as it doesn't come with a lot of added sugar and sodium.
• When the oatmeal is done, pass around samples in cups or make a breakfast buffet with skim milk, soy milk, and various fresh fruits.

Final question:
What are some of the benefits of fiber? How much fiber is in this breakfast? What kind of fiber?

Microwave Oatmeal

Ingredients:
1/2 cup rolled oats
1 cup water
1 tablespoon raisins
dash ground cinnamon
Place all ingredients in large cereal bowl. Microwave on 80% power for 3 minutes. Stir and serve.

Make It MyPlate:
• Skim milk, fresh orange

Ingredient List:
oatmeal (old fashioned)
raisins
cinnamon
skim milk
fresh orange

Optional: Various boxes of cold cereals and types of oatmeal for label comparisons.

Equipment List:
Measuring cups and spoons
large bowl
microwave oven
spoon
serving plate for fruit

Paper Goods and Misc:
Plates, napkins, and forks for tasting
Paper towels for kitchen cleanup
Baggies and plastic cups for ingredients
Cleaning supplies for kitchen sanitation

Breakfast Lesson

Handouts:
- MyPlate, MyPlate Shopping List, Breakfast, Recipe

Label reading lesson:
- Compare boxed cereal mixes and instant oatmeal packs to muesli. Draw attention to fiber and sodium content.
- Compare this muesli to pastries from Dunkin' Donuts and McDonalds. Discuss the huge differences in calories and fat. Remind the group that most large muffins, Danish, bagels, and breakfast pastries contain more than 400 calories apiece.

Get Organized - To Do Lists:

What to do ahead of time:
- Copy all handouts.
- Make printouts of some of the nutrition facts for breakfast foods from popular restaurant websites. We recommend McDonalds.com, Starbucks.com and DunkinDonuts.com.
- Measure all ingredients and place them in plastic bags or cups.

Start class:
- Greet the class and distribute handouts.
- Ask how many eat breakfast in the morning. Explain that today we are going to try muesli. Muesli means "mix" and is served in Switzerland for breakfast. It is a delicious and easy treat.

During class:
- Mix muesli according to directions and present in an attactive way.
- Explain that the muesli can be made up to 1 day ahead of time - and is easy to eat from a cup with a spoon when you're on the go. It also makes a great dessert or snack.

Final question:
What are some of the benefits of fiber? How much fiber is in this breakfast? What kind of fiber?

Muesli

Ingredients:
1/4 cup uncooked oatmeal
1/4 cup skim milk
3/4 cup light nonfat yogurt
1 cup assorted chopped fruits: apples, oranges, grapes, raisins
Ground cinnamon to taste
Optional: 1 tsp chopped walnuts

Directions:
Mix the oatmeal in a mixing bowl with the skim milk. Add the rest of the ingredient except for the walnuts. Place in large bowl or footed glasses and then sprinkle with nuts (serves 2 for breakfast or up to 10 for tasting).

Make It MyPlate:
- hot tea or a fat-free latte

Ingredient List:
Oatmeal
Skim milk
Light, nonfat yogurt
2 or more fresh fruits: apple, orange, grapes, pears, berries, dried fruits
Walnuts
Ground cinnamon

Optional: Various types of oatmeal and cold creals for label reading comparison

Equipment List:
Measuring cups and spoons
Knife
Cutting board
Mixing bowl
Serving spoon
Attractive large serving bowl or footed cups

Paper Goods and Misc:
Plates, napkins, and forks for tasting
Paper towels for kitchen cleanup
Baggies and plastic cups for ingredients
Cleaning supplies for kitchen sanitation

Breakfast Lesson

Handouts:
• MyPlate, MyPlate Shopping List, Breakfast, Recipe

Label reading lesson:
• Compare the cost and nutrient content of this egg white sandwich recipe to various breakfast offerings from McDonalds, Burger King and Dunkin' Donuts.

Get Organized - To Do Lists:

What to do ahead of time:
• Copy all handouts.
• Make printouts of some of the nutrition facts for breakfast foods from popular restaurant websites. We recommend McDonalds.com, Starbucks.com and DunkinDonuts.com.
• Measure all ingredients and place them in plastic bags or cups.

Start class:
• Greet the class and distribute handouts.
• Ask how many people in the group eat breakfast in the morning.

During class:
• Make the sandwich, then present it a plate. Garnish with a fresh fruit salad.
• Demonstrate how to wrap the sandwich in paper towels. This will make it easy to take it with you. You can also put the fruit in a plastic bag for a mid-morning snack.

Final question:
What are some of the benefits of fiber? How much fiber is in this breakfast? What kind of fiber?

Egg White Sandwich

Ingredients:
2 slices whole wheat bread, toasted
1 slice lowfat American cheese
1/2 cup egg white or nonfat egg substitute
low-sodium ketchup
black pepper
Directions: While bread is toasting, place egg white/substitute in large cereal bowl and microwave on high until done, about 2 to 3 minutes. Place egg substitute on top of toast; top with black pepper, cheese and ketchup; place final slice of toast. Serves 1 for breakfast or 4 for tastings.

Make It MyPlate:
• Fresh fruit, hot tea

Ingredient List:
Egg white or nonfat egg substitute
Whole wheat bread
Low sodium ketchup
Black pepper
Lowfat American cheese
Fresh fruit

Optional: Frozen breakfast sandwiches and pastries for nutrition facts comparison; regular ketchup to compare labels to regular ketchup

Equipment List:
Measuring cups and spoons
Knife
Cutting board
Large cereal bowl
Toaster
Microwave oven
Serving spoon
Attractive dinner plate

Paper Goods and Misc:
Plates, napkins, and forks for tasting
Paper towels for kitchen cleanup
Baggies and plastic cups for ingredients
Cleaning supplies for kitchen sanitation

Breakfast Lesson

Handouts:
• MyPlate, MyPlate Shopping List, Breakfast, Recipe

Label reading lesson:
• Compare this smoothie to others from from Dunkin Donuts and McDonalds. Discuss the huge differences in calories and fat.

Get Organized - To Do Lists:

What to do ahead of time:
• Copy all handouts.
• Make printouts of some of the nutrition facts for breakfast foods from popular restaurant websites. We recommend McDonalds.com, Starbucks.com and DunkinDonuts.com.
• Measure all ingredients and place them in plastic bags or cups.

Start class:
• Greet the class and distribute handouts.
• Ask how many in the group typically eat breakfast in the morning.
• Explain that this recipe is fast and creamy. It almost always gets you out the door with a smile. It's also a great way to use up extra fruit - simply freeze and use as needed for smoothies.

During class:
• Make the smoothie and pour it into a tall glass or to-go cup.
• If time and budget allow, it is fun to allow a few people (or everyone!) to make their own flavor concoctions. How about banana and nutmeg? Or strawberries with grated orange zest? Or blueberry and vanilla? Or peaches with almond extract?

Final question:
How does this recipe help you reach your MyPlate nutrition goals?

Sunrise Smoothie

Ingredients:
1 cup frozen fruit (berries and/or bananas)
1 cup skim milk
3 tablespoons oatmeal
pinch ground cinnamon
Directions:
Pour all ingredients a blender and blend on full power until smooth. Enjoy! Serves 1 for breakfast or 4 for tasting.

Make It MyPlate:
• Whole wheeat toast with jam

Ingredient List:
Frozen fruit
Skim milk
Ground cinnamon
Oatmeal

Optional: Bring several types of milk for label comparisons

Equipment List:
Measuring cups and spoons
Blender
Large glass for presentation

Paper Goods and Misc:
Plates, napkins, and forks for tasting
Paper towels for kitchen cleanup
Baggies and plastic cups for ingredients
Cleaning supplies for kitchen sanitation

Handouts:
• MyPlate, MyPlate Shopping List, Breakfast, Recipe

Label reading lesson:
• Compare this pastry to pastries from Dunkin' Donuts and McDonalds. Discuss the huge differences in calories and fat. Remind the group that most large muffins, Danish, bagels, and breakfast pastries contain more than 400 calories apiece.

Get Organized - To Do Lists:

What to do ahead of time:
• Copy all handouts.
• Make printouts of some of the nutrition facts for breakfast foods from popular restaurant websites. We recommend McDonalds.com, Starbucks.com and DunkinDonuts.com.
• Measure all ingredients and place them in plastic bags or cups.

Start class:
• Greet the class and distribute handouts.
• Ask how many eat breakfast in the morning.

During class:
• Make this "healthy breakfast pastry"and present it on attractive plate. You can also pack it in plastic baggies or tupperware to take on the go.
• If time and budget allow, make a few varieties of this pastry. Use different nut butters and fruit combinations. Almond and peaches; peanut and banana; peanut and berries; jam with fruit. Allow participants to make their favorites - or enlist a few helpers to do the same. Cut up the slices into little pieces and allow everyone a few samples.

Final question:
What are some of the benefits of fiber? How much fiber is in this breakfast? What kind of fiber?

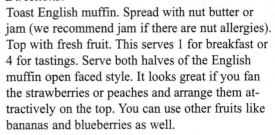

Breakfast Healthy Pastry: English Muffin Topped With Fruit

Ingredients:
English muffin (plain or whole wheat)
1 tablespoon nut butter or jam
1 cup fresh sliced fruit (berries and peaches)
Directions:
Toast English muffin. Spread with nut butter or jam (we recommend jam if there are nut allergies). Top with fresh fruit. This serves 1 for breakfast or 4 for tastings. Serve both halves of the English muffin open faced style. It looks great if you fan the strawberries or peaches and arrange them attractively on the top. You can use other fruits like bananas and blueberries as well.

Make It MyPlate: Fat-free light yogurt or skim milk or fat-free latte made with skim milk (use 1/2 cup milk, 1/2 cup brewed or instant coffee)

Ingredient List:
English muffin
Nut butter
Fresh fruits like peaches, berries and bananas

Optional: Various frozen and packaged pastries for label reading comparison - from the grocer's freezer and bakery and from the cereal aisle (e.g. Pop Tarts, Entenmann's Coffee Cake, frozen pastries, etc)

Equipment List:
Measuring cups and spoons
Knife
Cutting board
Attractive plate

Paper Goods and Misc:
Plates, napkins, and forks for tasting
Paper towels for kitchen cleanup
Baggies and plastic cups for ingredients
Cleaning supplies for kitchen sanitation

Microwave Oatmeal

Ingredients:

1/2 cup rolled oats
1 cup water
1 tablespoon raisins
dash ground cinnamon

Place all ingredients in large cereal bowl. Microwave on 80% power for 3 minutes. Stir and serve.

Make It MyPlate:

• Skim milk, fresh orange

Ingredient List:	Equipment List:
oatmeal (old fashioned) raisins cinnamon skim milk fresh orange Optional: Various boxes of cold cereals and types of oatmeal for label comparisons.	Measuring cups and spoons large bowl microwave oven spoon serving plate for fruit **Paper Goods and Misc:** Plates, napkins, and forks for tasting Paper towels for kitchen cleanup Baggies and plastic cups for ingredients Cleaning supplies for kitchen sanitation

Muesli

Ingredients:

1/4 cup uncooked oatmeal
1/4 cup skim milk
3/4 cup light nonfat yogurt
1 cup assorted chopped fruits: apples, oranges, grapes, raisins
Ground cinnamon to taste
Optional: 1 tsp chopped walnuts

Directions:

Mix the oatmeal in a mixing bowl with the skim milk. Add the rest of the ingredient except for the walnuts. Place in large bowl or footed glasses and then sprinkle with nuts (serves 2 for breakfast or up to 10 for tasting).

Make It MyPlate:

• hot tea or fat-free latte

Ingredient List:	Equipment List:
Oatmeal Skim milk Light, nonfat yogurt 2 or more fresh fruits: apple, orange, grapes, pears, berries, dried fruits Walnuts Ground cinnamon Optional: Various types of oatmeal and cold creals for label reading comparison	Measuring cups and spoons Knife Cutting board Mixing bowl Serving spoon Attractive large serving bowl or footed cups **Paper Goods and Misc:** Plates, napkins, and forks for tasting Paper towels for kitchen cleanup Baggies and plastic cups for ingredients Cleaning supplies for kitchen sanitation

Egg White Sandwich

Ingredients:

2 slices whole wheat bread, toasted

1 slice lowfat American cheese

1/2 cup egg white or nonfat egg substitute

low-sodium ketchup

black pepper

ChooseMyPlate.gov

Directions: While bread is toasting, place egg white/substitute in large cereal bowl and microwave on high until done, about 2 to 3 minutes. Place egg substitute on top of toast; top with black pepper, cheese and ketchup; place final slice of toast. Serves 1 for breakfast or 4 for tastings.

Make It MyPlate:
• Fresh fruit, hot tea

Ingredient List:	Equipment List:
Egg white or nonfat egg substitute	Measuring cups and spoons
Whole wheat bread	Knife
Low sodium ketchup	Cutting board
Black pepper	Large cereal bowl
Lowfat American cheese	Toaster
Fresh fruit	Microwave oven
	Serving spoon
Optional: Frozen breakfast sandwiches and pastries for nutrition facts comparison; regular ketchup to compare labels to regular ketchup	Attractive dinner plate
	Paper Goods and Misc:
	Plates, napkins, and forks for tasting
	Paper towels for kitchen cleanup
	Baggies and plastic cups for ingredients
	Cleaning supplies for kitchen sanitation

Sunrise Smoothie

Ingredients:

1 cup frozen fruit (berries and or bananas

1 cup skim milk

3 tablespoons oatmeal

pinch ground cinnamon

ChooseMyPlate.gov

Directions:

Pour all ingredients a blender and blend on full power until smooth. Enjoy! Serves 1 for breakfast or 4 for tasting.

Make It MyPlate:
• Whole wheast toast with jam

Ingredient List:	Equipment List:
Frozen fruit	Measuring cups and spoons
Skim milk	Blender
Ground cinnamon	Large glass for presentation
Oatmeal	
	Paper Goods and Misc:
Optional: Bring several types of milk for label comparisons	Plates, napkins, and forks for tasting
	Paper towels for kitchen cleanup
	Baggies and plastic cups for ingredients
	Cleaning supplies for kitchen sanitation

Breakfast Healthy Pastry: English Muffin Topped With Fruit

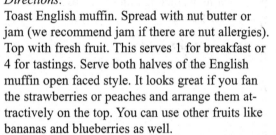

Choose**MyPlate**.gov

Ingredients:

English muffin (plain or whole wheat)

1 tablespoon nut butter or jam

1 cup fresh sliced fruit (berries and peaches)

Directions:

Toast English muffin. Spread with nut butter or jam (we recommend jam if there are nut allergies). Top with fresh fruit. This serves 1 for breakfast or 4 for tastings. Serve both halves of the English muffin open faced style. It looks great if you fan the strawberries or peaches and arrange them attractively on the top. You can use other fruits like bananas and blueberries as well.

Make It MyPlate: Fat-free light yogurt or skim milk or fat-free latte made with skim milk (use 1/2 cup milk, 1/2 cup brewed or instant coffee)

Ingredient List:

English muffin
Nut butter
Fresh fruits like peaches, berries and bananas

Optional: Various frozen and packaged pastries for label reading comparison - from the grocer's freezer and bakery and from the cereal aisle (e.g. Pop Tarts, Entenmann's Coffee Cake, frozen pastries, etc)

Equipment List:

Measuring cups and spoons
Knife
Cutting board
Attractive plate

Paper Goods and Misc:

Plates, napkins, and forks for tasting
Paper towels for kitchen cleanup
Baggies and plastic cups for ingredients
Cleaning supplies for kitchen sanitation

© Food & Health Communications *www.foodandhealth.com*

Have MyPlate for Breakfast

True or false: if you are trying to lose weight, it is a good idea to skip breakfast on most mornings.

Answer: False! Studies show that if you skip breakfast, you may very well make up for it by consuming more calories during the day and by binging on high-calorie snacks.

Benefits of breakfast:
- Breakfast is a great opportunity to increase your consumption of fiber, whole grains, fruit, and lowfat dairy.
- Having breakfast every morning kick starts your metabolism.
- A healthy breakfast not only gives you energy, but also increases cognitive function.
- Eating breakfast helps you regulate your calorie intake.
- When you eat a healthy breakfast, you are less likely to binge on high-calorie foods like donuts or vending machine snacks.

Try these healthy breakfast foods:
- High-fiber, whole-grain cereals
- Nutrient-rich fruits like bananas and oranges
- Fruit and whole grains are great sources of soluble fiber, which helps lower cholesterol.
- Calcium-rich skim milk was part of the DASH diet that successfully lowered blood pressure.

MyPlate recommends:
- Nonfat/low fat milk or calcium-fortified soy milk
- Lowfat and low sugar yogurt
- Fresh, seasonal fruit or 100% fruit juice
- Small portions of heart-healthy nuts
- A side of exercise

Breakfast.....
- is a habit of people who lose weight.
- helps you eat less during the day.
- is associated with a healthful BMI.
- is an excellent opportunity to get in more MyPlate food groups

No time for breakfast?
- Make food the night before you need it.
- Keep ingredients on hand for quick and healthy meals.
- Wake up 15 minutes earlier.

Not hungry enough for breakfast?
- Wake up earlier. That way, you're more likely to be hungry before you leave for the day.
- Exercise in the morning and build up an appetite.
- Make a breakfast that travels well (like a breakfast sandwich or a smoothie) and take it with you.

Would you rather get more sleep?
- Go to bed earlier
- Eat healthier
- Exercise (it helps you sleep better)
- Take your breakfast with you

Snack Lesson

Handouts:
• MyPlate, Snacks, Recipe

Label reading lesson:
• Compare fat, calories, fiber and sodium in this recipe to foods that are packaged and marketed as convenient snacks.
• Compare the calories per ounce for the packaged snacks versus the one in this recipe.

Get Organized - To Do Lists:

What to do ahead of time:
• Copy all handouts.
• Measure and chop all ingredients. Place them in plastic bags or cups.

Start class:
• Greet the class and distribute handouts.
• Ask how many people eat snacks? What did they eat for their last snack?
• Explain the importance of eating many small meals throughout the day to spread calories out throughout the day. It is also vital to eat when you're hungry, not out of boredom.
• Explain the importance of portion control when eating packaged snack foods. How easy would it be to eat an entire package of Ruffles potato chips while watching the Super Bowl?

During class:
• Prepare the parfaits.
• Ask for volunteers to help serve and distribute the snacks (remind them to wash their hands first).
• While people are eating, explain the MyPlate groups you are presenting and offer label comparisons for similar packaged foods that are high in fat and calories.

Final question:
Which food groups did we use today? Are there other healthy ways to combine these groups?

Yogurt Parfait

Ingredients:
1 cup nonfat, light yogurt
1/2 cup fresh fruit or fruit canned in water
2 tablespoons dry cereal (like Grapenuts)

Directions:
Layer yogurt, fruit and dry cereal in stemmed or footed dessert glass. Serves 1 for a snack or dessert or 4 for tastings.

Ingredient List:
Nonfat light yogurt
Fresh fruit
Cereal (Grapenuts)

Optional: various yogurts to compare labels and see how they can really vary in calories

Equipment List:
Measuring cups and spoons
Mixing bowl
Spoon
Footed glass for presentation

Paper Goods and Misc:
Plates, napkins, and forks for tasting
Paper towels for kitchen cleanup
Baggies and plastic cups for ingredients
Cleaning supplies for kitchen sanitation

Snack Lesson

Handouts:
• MyPlate, Snacks, Recipe

Label reading lesson:
• Compare fat, calories, fiber and sodium in this recipe to foods that are packaged and marketed as convenient snacks.
• Compare the calories per ounce for the packaged snacks versus the one in this recipe.

Get Organized - To Do Lists:

What to do ahead of time:
• Copy all handouts.
• Measure and chop all ingredients. Place them in plastic bags or cups.

Start class:
• Greet the class and distribute handouts.
• Ask how many people eat snacks? What did they eat for their last snack?
• Explain the importance of eating many small meals throughout the day to spread calories out throughout the day. It is also vital to eat when you're hungry, not out of boredom.
• Explain the importance of portion control when eating packaged snack foods. How easy would it be to eat an entire package of Ruffles potato chips while watching the Super Bowl?

During class:
• Prepare the hummus and arrange the veggies and pitas around it on a large platter.
• Ask for volunteers to help serve and distribute the snacks (remind them to wash their hands first).
• While people are eating, explain the MyPlate groups you are presenting and offer label comparisons for similar packaged foods that are high in fat and calories.

Final question:
Which food groups did we use today? Are there other healthy ways to combine these groups?

Veggies and Hummus

Ingredients:
Baby carrots
Red pepper, sliced
Cucumber sticks
Celery sticks
Raw broccoli
Hummus (prepared or use recipe below)
Whole wheat pita pockets (4) cut in triangles
Directions:
Arrange vegetables and pita triangles on large platter. Place the hummus in the center to use as a dip.
Hummus recipe - can make from scratch - use one can of drained garbanzo beans, juice of one lemon, 1 tablespoon olive oil, 2 cloves crushed garlic, black pepper to taste, 1 tsp cumin.

Make It MyPlate:
Add a protein and fruit with the veggies, hummus and pita pocket for a complete meal.

Ingredient List:
Baby carrots
Red pepper
Cucumber
Celery
Broccoli
Prepared hummus
Whole wheat pita pockets

Optional: Chips and packaged snacks to compare calories, fat and sodium.

For a light meal, serve raw veggies, hummus and pita triangles along with a tossed salad.

Equipment List:
Measuring cups and spoons
Knife
Cutting board
Bowl for hummus
Attractive plate

Paper Goods and Misc:
Plates, napkins, and forks for tasting
Paper towels for kitchen cleanup
Baggies and plastic cups for ingredients
Cleaning supplies for kitchen sanitation

Snack Lesson

Handouts:
- MyPlate, Snacks, Recipe

Label reading lesson:
- Compare fat, calories, fiber and sodium in this recipe to foods that are packaged and marketed as convenient snacks.
- Compare the calories per ounce for the packaged snacks versus the one in this recipe.

Get Organized - To Do Lists:

What to do ahead of time:
- Copy all handouts.
- Measure and chop all ingredients. Place them in plastic bags or cups.

Start class:
- Greet the class and distribute handouts.
- Ask how many people eat snacks? What did they eat for their last snack?
- Explain the importance of eating many small meals throughout the day to spread calories out throughout the day. It is also vital to eat when you're hungry, not out of boredom.
- Explain the importance of portion control when eating packaged snack foods. How easy would it be to eat an entire package of Ruffles potato chips while watching the Super Bowl?

During class:
- Arrange the fruit on a large platter.
- Ask for volunteers to help serve and distribute the snacks (remind them to wash their hands first).
- While people are eating, explain the MyPlate group you are presenting and offer label comparisons for similar packaged foods that are high in fat and calories.

Final question:
Which food group did we use today? What could we add to balance the plate?

Fresh fruit platter

Ingredients:
2 cups fresh cubed melon
2 cups fresh berries
2 oranges, peeled and cut in sections
2 pears, cored and cubed
2 cups red seedless grapes
1 cup dried cranberries or cherries or blueberries

Directions:
Place fruits on an attractive platter in sections. Try to alternate brightly colored fruits with less colorful items. Sprinkle with dried fruit.

Make It MyPlate:
This makes a fabulous fruit item for everyone to create a MyPlate meal - add veggies, lean protein and a whole grain.

Ingredient List:
Melon
Berries
Oranges
Pears
Grapes
Dried fruit
3 jars babyfood apricots
Vanilla nonfat light yogurt

Optional: Bag of cookies - show how much fruit you get to eat for 100 calories versus 100 calories of cookies. The fruit contains fiber and has little fat or sodium.

Equipment List:
Measuring cups and spoons
Knife
Cutting board
Bowls for dip
Attractive dinner plate

Paper Goods and Misc:
Plates, napkins, and forks for tasting
Paper towels for kitchen cleanup
Baggies and plastic cups for ingredients
Cleaning supplies for kitchen sanitation

Snack Lesson

Handouts:
• MyPlate, Snacks, Recipe

Label reading lesson:
• Compare fat, calories, fiber and sodium in this recipe to foods that are packaged and marketed as convenient snacks.
• Compare the calories per ounce for the packaged snacks versus the one in this recipe.

Get Organized - To Do Lists:

What to do ahead of time:
• Copy all handouts.
• Measure and chop all ingredients. Place them in plastic bags or cups.

Start class:
• Greet the class and distribute handouts.
• Ask how many people eat snacks? What did they eat for their last snack?
• Explain the importance of eating many small meals throughout the day to spread calories out throughout the day. It is also vital to eat when you're hungry, not out of boredom.
• Explain the importance of portion control when eating packaged snack foods. How easy would it be to eat an entire package of Ruffles potato chips while watching the Super Bowl?

During class:
• Prepare the salsa and arrange the veggies and chips around it on a large platter.
• Ask for volunteers to help serve and distribute the snacks (remind them to wash their hands first).
• While people are eating, explain the MyPlate groups you are presenting and offer label comparisons for similar packaged foods that are high in fat and calories.

Final question:
Which food groups did we use today? Are there other healthy ways to combine these groups?

Fresh Salsa

Ingredients:
6 plum tomatoes, cored and halved
1 onion, peeled and cut in wedges
Mild pepper, cored and cubed
2 tablespoons chopped cilantro
Juice of one lime
Directions:
Preheat broiler in oven or toaster oven. Arrange tomatoes, onions and peppers in single layer on baking tray and broil til very brown, about 15 minutes. Tray should be about 6 inches from heat source. Place onion, pepper, cilantro and lime in food processor and pulse until fine. Add tomatoes and pulse til chunky. Place in bowl and chill until ready to serve.

Make It MyPlate:
Salsa is a veggie - add a grain or fruit and a little protein like bean dip.

Ingredient List:	Equipment List:
6 plum tomatoes	Measuring cups and spoons
1 yellow or sweet onion	Knife
1 bunch cilantro (or can use parsley)	Cutting board
1 lime	Food processor
1 mild pepper	Broiler (oven or toaster oven)
Fresh veggies	Baking pan or dish - large
Baked corn chips	Attractive platter and bowl for salsa and dippers
Optional: Compare calories in baked versus fried chips. Compare sodium in this recipe versus bought salsa - the latter is much higher in sodium!	**Paper Goods and Misc:** Plates, napkins, and forks for tasting Paper towels for kitchen cleanup Baggies and plastic cups for ingredients Cleaning supplies for kitchen sanitation

---

Snack Lesson

Handouts:
• MyPlate, Snacks, Recipe

Label reading lesson:
• Compare fat, calories, fiber and sodium in this recipe to foods that are packaged and marketed as convenient snacks.
• Compare the calories per ounce for the packaged snacks versus the one in this recipe.

Get Organized - To Do Lists:

What to do ahead of time:
• Copy all handouts.
• Measure and chop all ingredients. Place them in plastic bags or cups.

Start class:
• Greet the class and distribute handouts.
• Ask how many people eat snacks? What did they eat for their last snack?
• Explain the importance of eating many small meals throughout the day to spread calories out throughout the day. It is also vital to eat when you're hungry, not out of boredom.
• Explain the importance of portion control when eating packaged snack foods. How easy would it be to eat an entire package of Ruffles potato chips while watching the Super Bowl?

During class:
• Prepare the sweet potatoes. Cut into smaller pieces for taste samples.
• Ask for volunteers to help serve and distribute the snacks (remind them to wash their hands first).
• While people are eating, explain the MyPlate groups you are presenting and offer label comparisons for similar packaged foods that are high in fat and calories.

Final question:
Which food groups did we use today? Are there other healthy ways to combine these groups?

Baked Sweet Potato

Ingredients:
1 sweet potato
1 tablespoon light margarine
1 tablespoon reduced calorie syrup
pinch cinnamon

Directions:
Rinse sweet potato to remove all dirt. Pierce sweet potato with a fork and bake in microwave until soft all the way through, about 5-6 minutes. Cut in half, fluff with a fork and fill with margarine and syrup; top with a pinch of ground cinnamon.

Make It MyPlate:
This veggie can be paired with baked chicken, fish or lean meat, whole grain pasta or brown rice and a fruit.

Ingredient List:
Sweet potato
Light margarine
Reduced calorie syrup
Pinch cinnamon

Optional: Compare a baked sweet potato with the fat and calories found in French fries and potato chips!

Equipment List:
Measuring cups and spoons
Knife
Fork
Microwave oven
Attractive dinner plate

Paper Goods and Misc:
Plates, napkins, and forks for tasting
Paper towels for kitchen cleanup
Baggies and plastic cups for ingredients
Cleaning supplies for kitchen sanitation

Healthful Snack Guide

Stock Your Kitchen Right

Having the right food on hand is very important for making fast, healthy snacks. If your snacks are based on whole grains, fruits and vegetables, with a little dairy and lean protein, you will be on your way to better health. Of course you will want to watch your intake of salt and saturated fat to keep your heart healthy. Here are some items you may want to keep on hand:

Grains:
- Low-fat, whole-grain crackers
- Whole-wheat pita bread (100%)
- Whole-wheat bread (100%)
- Baked tortilla chips
- Whole grain cereal

Vegetables:
- Raw vegetables
- Salads
- Potatoes and sweet potatoes
- Vegetable juice (100%)
- Vegetable soups

Fruits:
- Fresh fruit
- Dried fruit
- Fruit juice (100%)

Heart-Healthy Protein:
- Nuts and nut butters
- Bean dip

- Bean soup
- Bean salad
- Baked tofu
- Canned tuna or salmon
- White chicken or turkey, skinless

Heart Healthy Dairy:
- Nonfat, light yogurt
- Fortified soymilk and skim milk

Easy Snack Ideas

For healthy snacks, think *out with the bag* -- that is, out with foods that are sold as snacks in all those cute packages and bags. Refined carbohydrates such as pretzels, crackers, cookies and chips are often high in sodium and fat, and low in fiber. They are all calorie-dense as compared to the foods above and overconsumption of these can lead to weight gain. Eating healthy snacks is especially important if you are trying to watch your weight, lower your blood pressure and/or control your blood sugar. Here are some healthy, delicious snack ideas:

- **Peanut butter crackers** - An old standby is healthy when you place it on 100% whole grain, lowfat crackers (such as WASA brand crackers) or even 100% whole grain bread. If you are watching your weight, keep the peanut butter to 1 tablespoon per serving. You can always top with no-sugar-added preserves or fresh sliced fruit.
- **Soup** - Purchase low-sodium, low-fat vegetable or bean soup. It can be microwaved in minutes in a coffee mug. If you are keeping this at the office, don't forget the can opener.
- **Rabbit bag** - Put a few raw veggies and fruits together in a zip lock bag. Use orange wedges, apple slices, raw cauliflower and raw carrots. The orange gives everything a nice fla-

vor and helps keep the apple slices from turning too brown.
- **Smoothie** - Blend skim milk, fruit and wheat germ to make a delicious drink that tastes like a milk shake.
- **Low-sodium vegetable juice** helps you get more veggies in your day.
- **Sandwiches** don't have to be just for lunch; they are great for snacks, too. Stuff a whole-wheat pita with turkey or beans, lettuce, tomato and a little vinegar and oil for a heart-healthy treat.
- **Tuna or salmon on toast** - Make a tuna or salmon salad with low-fat mayonnaise. Spread it on 1 slice of toasted 100% whole wheat bread and top it with fresh sliced tomato and shredded romaine lettuce.
- **Cereal parfait** - Place light, nonfat yogurt, fruit and whole-grain cereal in a plastic cup and you will have a nutritious snack ready to go.
- **Baked sweet potato** - bake a sweet potato in the microwave and top it with reduced calorie pancake syrup and a pinch of cinnamon.

Calories per Serving:

Healthy Snacks	Calories
Broccoli	24
Carrots	52
Apple	81
Pear	97
Banana	108

High Calorie Snacks	Calories
Pretzel, soft	214
Cookie	260
Muffin	340
French fries	350
Cinnamon bun	370

Yogurt Parfait

Ingredients:
1 cup nonfat, light yogurt
1/2 cup fresh fruit or fruit canned in water
2 tablespoons dry cereal (Grapenuts)

ChooseMyPlate.gov

Directions:
Layer yogurt, fruit and dry cereal in stemmed or footed dessert glass. Serves 1 for a snack or dessert or 4 for tastings.

Make It MyPlate:
This is a snack that uses yogurt fruit and whole grains.

Ingredient List:	Equipment List:
Nonfat light yogurt Fresh fruit Cereal (Grapenuts) Optional: various yogurts to compare labels and see how they can really vary in calories	Measuring cups and spoons Mixing bowl Spoon Footed glass for presentation **Paper Goods and Misc:** Plates, napkins, and forks for tasting Paper towels for kitchen cleanup Baggies and plastic cups for ingredients Cleaning supplies for kitchen sanitation

Veggies and Hummus

Ingredients:
Baby carrots
Red pepper, sliced
Cucumber sticks
Celery sticks
Raw broccoli
Hummus (prepared or use recipe below)
Whole wheat pita pockets (4) cut in triangles

ChooseMyPlate.gov

Directions:
Arrange vegetables and pita triangles on large platter. Place the hummus in the center to use as a dip.
Hummus recipe - can make from scratch - use one can of drained garbanzo beans, juice of one lemon, 1 tablespoon olive oil, 2 cloves crushed garlic, black pepper to taste, 1 tsp cumin.

Make It MyPlate:
Turn it into a meal with lean protein and fruit.

Ingredient List:	Equipment List:
Baby carrots Red pepper Cucumber Celery Broccoli Prepared hummus Whole wheat pita pockets Optional: Chips and packaged snacks to compare calories, fat and sodium. For a light meal, serve raw veggies, hummus and pita triangles along with a tossed salad.	Measuring cups and spoons Knife Cutting board Bowl for hummus Attractive plate **Paper Goods and Misc:** Plates, napkins, and forks for tasting Paper towels for kitchen cleanup Baggies and plastic cups for ingredients Cleaning supplies for kitchen sanitation

Fresh fruit platter

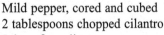

Ingredients:
2 cups fresh cubed melon
2 cups fresh berries
2 oranges, peeled and cut in sections
2 pears, cored and cubed
2 cups red seedless grapes
1 cup dried cranberries or cherries or blueberries

Directions:
Place fruits on an attractive platter in sections. Try to alternate brightly colored fruits with less colorful items. Sprinkle with dried fruit.

Make It MyPlate:
Use this platter for snacks or buffets so it can be a fruit that goes on 1/4 of the plate.

Ingredient List:	Equipment List:
Melon	Measuring cups and spoons
Berries	Knife
Oranges	Cutting board
Pears	Bowls for dip
Grapes	Attractive dinner plate
Dried fruit	
3 jars babyfood apricots	**Paper Goods and Misc:**
Vanilla nonfat light yogurt	Plates, napkins, and forks for tasting
	Paper towels for kitchen cleanup
Optional: Bag of cookies - show how much fruit you get to eat for 100 calories versus 100 calories of cookies. The fruit contains fiber and has little fat or sodium.	Baggies and plastic cups for ingredients Cleaning supplies for kitchen sanitation

Fresh Salsa

Ingredients:
6 plum tomatoes, cored and halved
1 onion, peeled and cut in wedges
Mild pepper, cored and cubed
2 tablespoons chopped cilantro
Juice of one lime

Directions:
Preheat broiler in oven or toaster oven. Arrange tomatoes, onions and peppers in single layer on baking tray and broil til very brown, about 15 minutes. Tray should be about 6 inches from heat source. Place onion, pepper, cilantro and lime in food processor and pulse until fine. Add tomatoes and pulse til chunky. Place in bowl and chill until ready to serve.

Make It MyPlate:
Add lean protein or beans, a whole grain and fruit.

Ingredient List:	Equipment List:
6 plum tomatoes	Measuring cups and spoons
1 yellow or sweet onion	Knife
1 bunch cilantro (or can use parsley)	Cutting board
1 lime	Food processor
1 mild pepper	Broiler (oven or toaster oven)
Fresh veggies	Baking pan or dish - large
Baked corn chips	Attractive platter and bowl for salsa and dippers
Optional: Compare calories in baked versus fried chips. Compare sodium in this recipe versus bought salsa - the latter is much higher in sodium!	**Paper Goods and Misc:** Plates, napkins, and forks for tasting Paper towels for kitchen cleanup Baggies and plastic cups for ingredients Cleaning supplies for kitchen sanitation

Baked Sweet Potato

ChooseMyPlate.gov

Ingredients:

1 sweet potato
1 tablespoon light margarine
1 tablespoon reduced calorie syrup
pinch cinnamon

Directions:

Rinse sweet potato to remove all dirt. Pierce sweet potato with a fork and bake in microwave until soft all the way through, about 5-6 minutes. Cut in half, fluff with a fork and fill with margarine and syrup; top with a pinch of ground cinnamon.

Make It MyPlate:

This veggie can be paired with a lean protein, a whole grain and fruit for a complete MyPlate meal.

Ingredient List:	Equipment List:
Sweet potato	Measuring cups and spoons
Light margarine	Knife
Reduced calorie syrup	Fork
Pinch cinnamon	Microwave oven
	Attractive dinner plate
Optional: Compare a baked sweet potato with the fat and calories found in French fries and potato chips!	**Paper Goods and Misc:**
	Plates, napkins, and forks for tasting
	Paper towels for kitchen cleanup
	Baggies and plastic cups for ingredients
	Cleaning supplies for kitchen sanitation

Kids MyPlate Lesson

Handouts:
• MyPlate, Recipe, Kids Activity Sheet

Label reading lesson:
• Bring in 2 boxes of cereal, whole milk and skim milk, potato chips, assorted fruits and veggies and candy bars to help the kids learn to read labels. Compare potato chips, candy bars and high-calorie foods with fruits and vegetables by calories per ounce along with fat, sodium and total calories.

Get Organized - To Do Lists:

What to do ahead of time:
• Copy all handouts.
• Measure and chop all ingredients. Place them in plastic bags or cups.
• If possible, set up stations so kids can help you make the poasta. Determine how many kids you will have for the class and divide them into groups.

Start class:
• Greet the class and distribute handouts.
• Ask how many help their parent(s) prepare dinner.

During class:
• Have everyone wash their hands. Explain the importance of hand washing and keeping food contact surfaces clean. Outline the importance of temperature - keep hot foods hot and cold foods cold. And be sure to say that once a utensil touches raw food, it should not come in contact with food that will not be heated.
• Divide the class into groups and give each group a station. If you do not have the resources to allow each kid to cook, bring up some volunteers to assist in cooking and passing things out.
• Assign kids for cleanup, passing out tastes, passing out handouts, storing food, and storing equipment.
• Prepare items in groups or use volunteers from the audience. Prepare food according to the recipe.
• Pass out tastes of food and gather feedback.

Final question:
How many food groups did we use today? How many servings from each one?

Pick A Pasta Shape

Ingredients:
1 cup broccoli tops
3 cups heated pasta sauce
2 cups dry small-shaped pasta (can be whole wheat)
Parmesan cheese (1 tablespoon)

Directions:
Cook pasta according to package directions and drain in colander. Steam broccoli in a covered bowl in the microwave. Heat the pasta sauce over the stove on medium heat, bringing to a boil slowly and stirring occasionally. Mix the heated pasta sauce with the cooked pasta and top with cheese. Serve broccoli to the side.

Serves 4. Makes enough tastings for 8. Each serving: 147 calories, .5 g fat, 0 g saturated fat, 0 g trans fat, 1 mg cholesterol, 260 mg sodium, 30 g carbohydrate, 7 g fiber, 7 g protein.

Make It MyPlate:
Add a lean protein and fruit.

Ingredient List:	Equipment List:
broccoli	Measuring cups and
tomatoes	spoons
pasta sauce	Knife
pasta (whole wheat)	Cutting board
	Microwave
Optional: Bring in various shapes of pasta to teach the names; allow kids to pick their favorite shape!	Stove top burner
	Colander
	Medium pot
	Cooking spoon
	Serving spoon
	Attractive dinner plate

Paper Goods and Misc:
Plates, napkins, and forks for tasting
Paper towels for kitchen cleanup
Baggies and plastic cups for ingredients
Cleaning supplies for kitchen sanitation

Kids MyPlate Lesson

Handouts:
• MyPlate, Recipe, Kids Activity Sheet

Label reading lesson:
• Bring in 2 boxes of cereal, whole milk and skim milk, potato chips, assorted fruits and veggies and candy bars to help the kids learn to read labels. Compare potato chips, candy bars and high-calorie foods with fruits and vegetables by calories per ounce along with fat, sodium and total calories.

Get Organized - To Do Lists:

What to do ahead of time:
• Copy all handouts.
• Measure and chop all ingredients. Place them in plastic bags or cups.
• If possible, set up stations so kids can help you make the poasta. Determine how many kids you will have for the class and divide them into groups.

Start class:
• Greet the class and distribute handouts.
• Ask how many help their parent(s) prepare dinner.

During class:
• Have everyone wash their hands. Explain the importance of hand washing and keeping food contact surfaces clean. Outline the importance of temperature - keep hot foods hot and cold foods cold. And be sure to say that once a utensil touches raw food, it should not come in contact with food that will not be heated.
• Divide the class into groups and give each group a station. If you do not have the resources to allow each kid to cook, bring up some volunteers to assist in cooking and passing things out.
• Assign kids for cleanup, passing out tastes, passing out handouts, storing food, and storing equipment.
• Prepare items in groups or use volunteers from the audience. Prepare food according to the recipe.
• Pass out tastes of food and gather feedback.

Make It MyPlate:
How many food groups did we use today? How many servings from each one? List your favorite protein, grain and fruit to complete the MyPlate dish.

Microwave Veggies

ChooseMyPlate.gov

Ingredients:
Corn on the cob with light margarine
Broccoli with lemon
Baby carrots with honey
Potatoes with fat-free sour cream

Directions:
• Husk the corn and wrap in plastic wrap; microwave for 3 minutes per ear. Serve with light margarine.
• Rinse the broccoli and place the tops in a covered dish; microwave on high for 3-4 minutes. Serve with lemon.
• Place the carrots in a microwaveable container; sprinkle with a little water; cover and microwave on high until tender, about 5 minutes. Serve with honey.
• Wash potatoes and pierce with fork. Microwave on high for 4-5 minutes per potato. Serve with fat-free sour cream.

Now kids have 4 different vegetables they can prepare with the microwave!

Ingredient List:
corn
light margarine
baby carrots
honey
broccoli
lemon
baking potatoes (medium)
fat-free sourcream

Optional: Compare the fat in different kinds of margarine. Compare the fat in regular versus fat-free sour cream. Compare the sodium in fresh versus canned vegetables.

Equipment List:
Measuring cups and spoons
Knife
Cutting board
Microwave
Microwave containers
Serving spoon
Attractive dinner plates

Paper Goods and Misc:
Plates, napkins, and forks for tasting
Paper towels for kitchen cleanup
Baggies and plastic cups for ingredients
Cleaning supplies for kitchen sanitation

Kids MyPlate Lesson

Handouts:
• MyPlate, Recipe, Kids Activity Sheet

Label reading lesson:
• Bring in 2 boxes of cereal, whole milk and skim milk, potato chips, assorted fruits and veggies and candy bars to help the kids learn to read labels. Compare potato chips, candy bars and high-calorie foods with fruits and vegetables by calories per ounce along with fat, sodium and total calories.

Get Organized - To Do Lists:

What to do ahead of time:
• Copy all handouts.
• Measure and chop all ingredients. Place them in plastic bags or cups.
• If possible, set up stations so kids can help you make the poasta. Determine how many kids you will have for the class and divide them into groups.

Start class:
• Greet the class and distribute handouts.
• Ask how many help their parent(s) prepare dinner.

During class:
• Have everyone wash their hands. Explain the importance of hand washing and keeping food contact surfaces clean. Outline the importance of temperature - keep hot foods hot and cold foods cold. And be sure to say that once a utensil touches raw food, it should not come in contact with food that will not be heated.
• Divide the class into groups and give each group a station. If you do not have the resources to allow each kid to cook, bring up some volunteers to assist in cooking and passing things out.
• Assign kids for cleanup, passing out tastes, passing out handouts, storing food, and storing equipment.
• Prepare items in groups or use volunteers from the audience. Prepare food according to the recipe.
• Pass out tastes of food and gather feedback.

Final question:
How many food groups did we use today? How many servings from each one?

Healthy Mac and Cheese

Ingredients:
1 box macaroni and cheese mix
2 tablespoons grated carrot
1/4 cup skim milk
Peas with light margarine

Directions:
Cook macaroni in plenty of boiling water until tender, about 5 minutes. Drain and reserve in colander.
Grate carrot into the same sauce pan. Add the milk and bring to a boil. Lower to simmer for 1 minute and then add the cooked macaroni and half the cheese mix. Serve hot. Meanwhile, heat the peas and serve on the side.
Serves 4 or makes 8 tastings. Each serving: 323 calories, 6 g fat, 3.5 g saturated fat, 0 g trans fat, 16 mg cholesterol, 297 mg sodium, 49 g carbohydrates, 16 g protein.

Make It MyPlate:
Add veggies, lean protein and fruit to this fun and favorite grain dish that is made healthier.

Ingredient List:	Equipment List:
1 box mac and cheese mix	Measuring cups and spoons
1 carrot	Stove top burner (can use portable one)
Skim milk	Medium pans
Frozen peas	Colander
Light margarine for peas	Grater
	Cooking spoon
Optional: Compare prepared macaroni and cheese mix with this recipe; compare regular milk with skim milk. Make a large salad to go with this dish.	Serving spoon
	Attractive dinner plate

Paper and Misc:
Plates, napkins, and forks for tasting
Paper towels for kitchen cleanup
Baggies and plastic cups for ingredients
Cleaning supplies for kitchen sanitation

Kids MyPlate Lesson

Handouts:
• MyPlate, Recipe, Kids Activity Sheet

Label reading lesson:
• Bring in 2 boxes of cereal, whole milk and skim milk and candy bars to learn to read labels. Compare potato chips, candy bars and high-calorie foods with fruits and vegetables by calories per ounce along with fat, sodium and total calories.

Get Organized - To Do Lists:

What to do ahead of time:
• Copy all handouts.
• Measure and chop all ingredients. Place them in plastic bags or cups.
• If possible, set up stations so kids can help. Determine how many kids you will have for the class and how many groups and kids per group.

Start class:
• Greet the class and distribute handouts.
• Ask how many help their parent(s) prepare dinner.

During class:
• Have everyone wash their hands. Explain the importance of hand washing and keeping food contact surfaces clean. Explain the importance of temperature - keep hot foods hot and cold foods cold. And explain that once a utensil touches raw food it should not come in contact with food that will not be heated.
• Divide the class into groups and give each group a station. If you do not have the resources to allow each kid to cook, bring up some volunteers to assist in cooking and passing things out.
• Make job assignments to kids for cleanup, passing out tastes, passing out handouts, storing food and putting away equipment.
• Prepare items in groups or use volunteers from the audience. Prepare food according to the recipe.
• Pass out tastes of food and gather feedback.

Final question:
How many food groups did we use today? How many servings from each one?

Pizza

Ingredients:
4 whole wheat flour tortillas
2 cups pasta sauce (no added salt)
2 cups assorted fresh veggies
1 cup light mozzarella grated cheese

Directions:
Preheat oven to 350 degrees. Top tortillas with pasta sauce and a variety of fresh veggies - allow everyone to make their own concoction. Sprinkle lightly with light mozzarella cheese. Bake until veggies are heated through and cheese melts, about 10-15 minutes. Serve hot.
Serves 4 or (makes 16 tastings -cut each pizza in quarters for tasting). Each serving: 242 calories, 2 g fat, <1 g saturated fat, 0 g trans fat, 5 mg cholesterol, 481 mg sodium, 56 g carbohydrate, 12 g protein.

Make It MyPlate:
Pizza can count as a grain and veg. Add lean protein and fruit.

Ingredient List:	Equipment List:
Whole wheat flour tortillas	Measuring cups and spoons
Pasta sauce (low-sodium)	Knife
Fresh veggies: peppers, onions, mushrooms, tomatoes, green onion	Cutting board
Light mozzarella cheese	Baking pans
	Spatula
	Oven or toaster oven
	Attractive dinner plate

Paper Goods and Misc:

Optional: Compare frozen pizza to this recipe to save calories, sodium, fat and saturated fat.

Plates, napkins, and forks for tasting
Paper towels for kitchen cleanup
Baggies and plastic cups for ingredients
Cleaning supplies for kitchen sanitation

Kids MyPlate Lesson

Handouts:
• MyPlate, Recipe, Kids Activity Sheet

Label reading lesson:
• Bring in 2 boxes of cereal, whole milk and skim milk and candy bars to learn to read labels. Compare potato chips, candy bars and high-calorie foods with fruits and vegetables by calories per ounce along with fat, sodium and total calories.

Get Organized - To Do Lists:

What to do ahead of time:
• Copy all handouts.
• Measure and chop all ingredients. Place them in plastic bags or cups.
• If possible, set up stations so kids can help. Determine how many kids you will have for the class and how many groups and kids per group.

Start class:
• Greet the class and distribute handouts.
• Ask how many help their parent(s) prepare dinner.

During class:
• Have everyone wash their hands. Explain the importance of hand washing and keeping food contact surfaces clean. Explain the importance of temperature - keep hot foods hot and cold foods cold. And explain that once a utensil touches raw food it should not come in contact with food that will not be heated.
• Divide the class into groups and give each group a station. If you do not have the resources to allow each kid to cook, bring up some volunteers to assist in cooking and passing things out.
• Make job assignments to kids for cleanup, passing out tastes, passing out handouts, storing food and putting away equipment.
• Prepare items in groups or use volunteers from the audience. Prepare food according to the recipe.
• Pass out tastes of food and gather feedback.

Final question:
How many food groups did we use today? How many servings from each one?

Stir 'Em Stir Fry

Ingredients:
2 cups cooked brown rice
1 tablespoon oil
1 garlic clove
1 tablespoon grated ginger
4 cups fresh stir fry veggies
(broccoli, red pepper, mushrooms, carrots, celery)
2 tablespoons light soy sauce
Directions:
Add oil to a large nonstick skillet (or wok) and heat over medium-high stove. Saute garlic and ginger for about a minute then add the rest of the vegetables. Stir fry til crisp-tender, about 8 minutes. Season with soy sauce and serve over hot cooked rice.

Make It MyPlate:
This dish has veggies and a whole grain. Add a lean chicken and some fruit for a complete MyPlate meal.

Ingredient List:
Brown rice
Canola oil
Garlic
Ginger
Assorted fresh veggies:
broccoli, red pepper,
mushrooms, carrots,
celerty
Light soy sauce

Optional: Compare brown and white rice. Compare boxed rice mixes to plain rice for sodium content. Compare regular soy sauce to light soy sauce for sodium content.

Equipment List:
Measuring cups and spoons
Knife
Cutting board
Rice cooker
Stove top burner (can use portable one)
Nonstick skillet or wok
Cooking spoon
Serving spoon
Attractive dinner plate

Paper Goods and Misc:
Plates, napkins, and forks for tasting
Paper towels for kitchen cleanup
Baggies and plastic cups for ingredients
Cleaning supplies for kitchen sanitation

Kids MyPlate Lesson

Handouts:
• MyPlate, Recipe, Kids Activity Sheet

Label reading lesson:
• Bring in 2 boxes of cereal, whole milk and skim milk and candy bars to learn to read labels. Compare potato chips, candy bars and high-calorie foods with fruits and vegetables by calories per ounce along with fat, sodium and total calories.

Get Organized - To Do Lists:

What to do ahead of time:
• Copy all handouts.
• Measure and chop all ingredients. Place them in plastic bags or cups.
• If possible, set up stations so kids can help. Determine how many kids you will have for the class and how many groups and kids per group.

Start class:
• Greet the class and distribute handouts.
• Ask how many help their parent(s) prepare dinner.

During class:
• Have everyone wash their hands. Explain the importance of hand washing and keeping food contact surfaces clean. Explain the importance of temperature - keep hot foods hot and cold foods cold. And explain that once a utensil touches raw food it should not come in contact with food that will not be heated.
• Divide the class into groups and give each group a station. If you do not have the resources to allow each kid to cook, bring up some volunteers to assist in cooking and passing things out.
• Make job assignments to kids for cleanup, passing out tastes, passing out handouts, storing food and putting away equipment.
• Prepare items in groups or use volunteers from the audience. Prepare food according to the recipe.
• Pass out tastes of food and gather feedback.

Final question:
How many food groups did we use today? How many servings from each one?

Make Your Own Taco

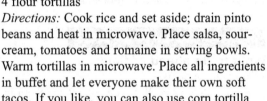

Ingredients:
2 cups cooked brown rice
1 can pinto beans
Prepared salsa
Fat-free sour cream
Chopped romaine lettuce
(washed and ready to serve)
1 cup chopped tomatoes
4 flour tortillas
Directions: Cook rice and set aside; drain pinto beans and heat in microwave. Place salsa, sour-cream, tomatoes and romaine in serving bowls. Warm tortillas in microwave. Place all ingredients in buffet and let everyone make their own soft tacos. If you like, you can also use corn tortilla shells.

Make It MyPlate:
This fun buffet uses a whole grain, protein (beans) and veggies. All you need is fruit!

Ingredient List:
Brown rice
Pinto beans
Salsa
Fat-free sour cream
Romaine lettuce
Ripe tomato
Whole grain flour tortillas

Optional: Compare these tacos with the ones in fast food places like Taco Bell for fat and saturated fat.

Check out the fiber content in pinto beans!

Equipment List:
Bowls for ingredients
Can opener
Knife
Cutting board
Rice cooker
Stove top burner (can use portable one)
Nonstick skillet
Cooking spoon
Serving spoon
Attractive dinner plate

Paper Goods and Misc:
Plates, napkins, and forks for tasting
Paper towels for kitchen cleanup
Baggies and plastic cups for ingredients
Cleaning supplies for kitchen sanitation

Kids MyPlate Lesson

Handouts:
• MyPlate, Recipe, Kids Activity Sheet

Label reading lesson:
• Bring in 2 boxes of cereal, whole milk and skim milk and candy bars to learn to read labels. Compare potato chips, candy bars and high-calorie foods with fruits and vegetables by calories per ounce along with fat, sodium and total calories.

Get Organized - To Do Lists:

What to do ahead of time:
• Copy all handouts.
• Measure and chop all ingredients. Place them in plastic bags or cups.
• If possible, set up stations so kids can help. Determine how many kids you will have for the class and how many groups and kids per group.

Start class:
• Greet the class and distribute handouts.
• Ask how many help their parent(s) prepare dinner.

During class:
• Have everyone wash their hands. Explain the importance of hand washing and keeping food contact surfaces clean. Explain the importance of temperature - keep hot foods hot and cold foods cold.
• Divide the class into groups and give each group a station. If you do not have the resources to allow each kid to cook, bring up some volunteers to assist in cooking and passing things out.
• Make job assignments to kids for cleanup, passing out tastes, passing out handouts, storing food and putting away equipment.
• Prepare items in groups or use volunteers from the audience. Prepare food according to the recipe.
• Pass out tastes of food and gather feedback.

Final question:
How many food groups did we use today? How many servings from each one? What else would you serve with your salad?

Salad for Kings and Queens

Ingredients:
Romaine lettuce (ready to serve)
Chopped tomatoes
Sliced peppers
Sliced green onions
Sliced cucumber
Baby carrots
Celery Sticks
Assorted flavored vinegars
Olive oil
Black pepper to taste
Assorted light salad dressings
Directions: Place the romaine lettuce in a large salad bowl. Top with chopped tomatoes, sliced peppers, green onions and cucumbers. Place the baby carrots and celery sticks in a vertical pattern like a king's crown around the edge of the bowl. Serve with assorted vinegars and dressings.

Make It MyPlate:
Use this salad for half or 1/4th of your plate with whole grain, protein and fruit.

Ingredient List:
Romaine lettuce
Ripe tomatoes
Bell pepper
Green onions
Cucumber
Baby carrots
Celery sticks
Flavored vinegar
Olive oil
Black pepper
Light dressing

Optional: Compare various salad dressings versus vinegar for sodium and fat content.

Equipment List:
Salad bowl and tongs
Knife
Cutting board
Cruet for oil
Attractive dinner plate

Paper Goods and Misc:
Plates, napkins, and forks for tasting
Paper towels for kitchen cleanup
Baggies and plastic cups for ingredients
Cleaning supplies for kitchen sanitation

Kids MyPlate Lesson

Handouts:
• MyPlate, Recipe, Kids Activity Sheet

Label reading lesson:
• Bring in 2 boxes of cereal, whole milk and skim milk and candy bars to learn to read labels. Compare potato chips, candy bars and high-calorie foods with fruits and vegetables by calories per ounce along with fat, sodium and total calories.

Get Organized - To Do Lists:

What to do ahead of time:
• Copy all handouts.
• Measure and chop all ingredients. Place them in plastic bags or cups.
• If possible, set up stations so kids can help. Determine how many kids you will have for the class and how many groups and kids per group.

Start class:
• Greet the class and distribute handouts.
• Ask how many help their parent(s) prepare dinner.

During class:
• Have everyone wash their hands. Explain the importance of hand washing and keeping food contact surfaces clean. Explain the importance of temperature - keep hot foods hot and cold foods cold. And explain that once a utensil touches raw food it should not come in contact with food that will not be heated.
• Divide the class into groups and give each group a station. If you do not have the resources to allow each kid to cook, bring up some volunteers to assist in cooking and passing things out.
• Make job assignments to kids for cleanup, passing out tastes, passing out handouts, storing food and putting away equipment.
• Prepare items in groups or use volunteers from the audience. Prepare food according to the recipe.
• Pass out tastes of food and gather feedback.

Final question:
How many food groups did we use today? How many servings from each one?

Baked Burgers and Fries

Ingredients:
3 baking potatoes
Cooking oil spray
Turkey burger patties
Lettuce
Tomato
Ketchup (low sodium)
Whole wheat bread

Directions:
Preheat oven to 450 degrees F. Cut potatoes in wedges and place on non-stick baking tray. Spray the top of the potatoes with the cooking spray. Bake until crispy on the bottom side, about 14 minutes then flip over and bake until crispy on the other side, about 5 minutes. Meanwhile, bake the burger patties. Serve the patties with the lettuce, tomato and whole grain bread. Garnish with drizzles of ketchup.

Make It MyPlate:
Here you have protein, a whole grain and veggies. Add your favorite fruit!

Ingredient List:
Potatoes
Cooking oil spray
Turkey burger patties
Lettuce
Tomato
Ketchup (low sodium)
Whole wheat bread

Optional: Compare recipe to nutrition facts for fast food burgers and fries.

Equipment List:
Knife
Cutting board
Oven
Baking trays
Spatula
Serving spoon
Attractive dinner plate

Paper Goods and Misc:
Plates, napkins, and forks for tasting
Paper towels for kitchen cleanup
Baggies and plastic cups for ingredients
Cleaning supplies for kitchen sanitation

Kids MyPlate Lesson

Handouts:
• MyPlate, Recipe, Kids Activity Sheet

Label reading lesson:
• Bring in 2 boxes of cereal, whole milk and skim milk and candy bars to learn to read labels. Compare potato chips, candy bars and high-calorie foods with fruits and vegetables by calories per ounce along with fat, sodium and total calories.

Get Organized - To Do Lists:

What to do ahead of time:
• Copy all handouts.
• Measure and chop all ingredients. Place them in plastic bags or cups.
• If possible, set up stations so kids can help. Determine how many kids you will have for the class and how many groups and kids per group.

Start class:
• Greet the class and distribute handouts.
• Ask how many help their parent(s) prepare dinner.

During class:
• Have everyone wash their hands. Explain the importance of hand washing and keeping food contact surfaces clean. Explain the importance of temperature - keep hot foods hot and cold foods cold. And explain that once a utensil touches raw food it should not come in contact with food that will not be heated.
• Divide the class into groups and give each group a station. If you do not have the resources to allow each kid to cook, bring up some volunteers to assist in cooking and passing things out.
• Make job assignments to kids for cleanup, passing out tastes, passing out handouts, storing food and putting away equipment.
• Prepare items in groups or use volunteers from the audience. Prepare food according to the recipe.
• Pass out tastes of food and gather feedback.

Final question:
How many food groups did we use today? How many servings from each one? Pick what you would serve with your potato bar!

Baked Potato Bar

Ingredients:
4 medium baking potatoes
2 cups broccoli tops
Light margarine
Fat-free sour cream
Diced tomato
Chopped green onion

Directions: Rinse dirt from potatoes and pierce with a fork. Bake potatoes in microwave for 4-5 minutes per potato. Meanwhile trim and rinse broccoli and place in covered bowl. Cut the tomatoes and green onions and place in bowls. When potatoes come out of the microwave, cook the broccoli in the covered bowl in the micrwave for 3-4 minutes or until tender. Cut the potatoes in half and serve all buffet style - allowing everyone to make their own baked stuffed potato!

Make It MyPlate:
This is an example of a great veggie. Pair with lean protein, a whole grain and some fruit.

Ingredient List:	**Equipment List:**
4 baking potatoes	Knife
1 stalk broccoli	Cutting board
Light margarine	Microwave
Fat-free sourcream	Bowls for ingredients
Ripe tomato	Serving spoons
Green onions	Fork to fluff potato
	Attractive dinner plate

Optional: Compare these potatoes to French fries. Compare light margarine to butter. Compare regular sour cream to fat-free sour cream.

Paper Goods and Misc:
Plates, napkins, and forks for tasting
Paper towels for kitchen cleanup
Baggies and plastic cups for ingredients
Cleaning supplies for kitchen sanitation

Kids MyPlate Lesson

Handouts:
• MyPlate, Recipe, Kids Activity Sheet

Label reading lesson:
• Bring in 2 boxes of cereal, whole milk and skim milk and candy bars to learn to read labels. Compare potato chips, candy bars and high-calorie foods with fruits and vegetables by calories per ounce along with fat, sodium and total calories.

Get Organized - To Do Lists:

What to do ahead of time:
• Copy all handouts.
• Measure and chop all ingredients. Place them in plastic bags or cups.
• If possible, set up stations so kids can help. Determine how many kids you will have for the class and how many groups and kids per group.

Start class:
• Greet the class and distribute handouts.
• Ask how many help their parent(s) prepare dinner.

During class:
• Have everyone wash their hands. Explain the importance of hand washing and keeping food contact surfaces clean. Explain the importance of temperature - keep hot foods hot and cold foods cold. And explain that once a utensil touches raw food it should not come in contact with food that will not be heated.
• Divide the class into groups and give each group a station. If you do not have the resources to allow each kid to cook, bring up some volunteers to assist in cooking and passing things out.
• Make job assignments to kids for cleanup, passing out tastes, passing out handouts, storing food and putting away equipment.
• Prepare items in groups or use volunteers from the audience. Prepare food according to the recipe.
• Pass out tastes of food and gather feedback.

Final question:
How many food groups did we use today? How many servings from each one?

Chicken and Veggie Sticks and Dip

ChooseMyPlate.gov

Ingredients:
Chicken tenders, 12 ounces
Barbecue sauce, 3 tablespoons
Baby carrots, 2 cups
Celery sticks, 1 cup
Broccoli tops, 1 cup
Light ranch dip, 1 cup
Directions: Place chicken tenders in a single layer in a glass microwaveable square baking pan. Lightly drizzle with barbecue sauce and cover with plastic wrap. Microwave on high for 5 minutes. Stir. Microwave until chicken is firm and done and no longer pink in the center, about 8 minutes total. Meanwhile, make a platter with the dip in the center and the raw veggies around it. Serve the hot chicken fingers with the veggies and dip.

Make It MyPlate:
This protein and veggie dish just needs a whole grain pita pocket and some fruit.

Ingredient List:
12 oz chicken tenders
Barbecue sauce
Baby carrots
Celery sticks
Broccoli tops
Light ranch dip

Optional: Serve with whole grain pita pockets (warmed). Compare this recipe to fried chicken fingers for calories, fat and sodium.

Equipment List:
Microwave
Knife
Cutting board
Baking dish
Bowl for dip
Serving platter

Paper Goods and Misc:
Plates, napkins, and forks for tasting
Paper towels for kitchen cleanup
Baggies and plastic cups for ingredients
Cleaning supplies for kitchen sanitation

MyPlate Word Search

```
N  Q  B  T  G  Y  C  B  G  A  I  S  S  B  L
F  C  C  V  Z  H  C  B  Z  T  A  B  N  E  I
E  S  I  C  R  E  X  E  T  L  T  M  I  A  O
M  P  V  G  V  I  A  Y  A  A  Y  P  A  N  M
P  X  E  D  I  X  R  D  O  P  E  Y  R  S  Z
Z  O  G  D  W  E  U  H  Y  G  C  M  G  N  O
X  Z  E  Y  Y  J  J  R  G  S  U  W  W  Z  A
P  W  T  Q  E  H  A  D  R  G  N  R  O  C  A
E  A  A  U  Z  M  T  M  R  I  D  D  T  U  Y
O  H  B  E  I  H  C  L  S  C  V  P  Z  H  R
V  A  L  D  H  Z  M  T  A  K  L  I  M  P  F
N  G  E  L  M  H  I  D  H  E  O  L  W  X  S
I  I  S  H  K  U  A  N  I  P  H  T  P  L  O
C  C  R  V  R  U  T  W  I  J  Z  G  W  S  I
H  V  Y  F  A  P  P  L  E  S  O  L  F  M  F
```

APPLES
BEANS
EXERCISE
FRUITS
GRAINS
HEALTHY
MEAT
MILK
MYPLATE
OIL
SALAD
VEGETABLES
YOGURT

Write the group that each food comes from.
Here are your group choices from MyPlate:
Grain, Vegetable, Fruit, Dairy, Protein

Bread   _____
Cereal   _____
Tuna   _____
Chicken   _____
Pinto Beans   _____
Broccoli   _____
Pears   _____
Grapes   _____
Yogurt   _____
Milk   _____
Steak   _____
Eggs   _____
Rice   _____
Oatmeal   _____
Carrots   _____
Tomatoes   _____
Lettuce   _____
Pasta   _____
Bananas   _____
Oranges   _____

Draw your favorite fruit and vegetable and color it in.

Circle the 5 food groups from MyPlate:

vegetables   eggs

potatoes   protein

grains   dairy

fruits   ice cream

vegetables   French fries

                    candy

ChooseMyPlate.gov

© Food & Health Communications www.foodandhealth.com

Pick A Pasta Shape

Ingredients:
1 cup broccoli tops
3 cups heated pasta sauce
2 cups dry, small-shaped pasta (can be whole wheat)
Parmesan cheese (1 tablespoon)

ChooseMyPlate.gov

Directions:
Cook pasta according to package directions and drain in colander. Steam broccoli in a covered bowl in the microwave. Heat the pasta sauce over the stove on medium heat, bringing to a boil slowly and stirring occasionally. Mix the heated pasta sauce with the cooked pasta and top with cheese. Serve broccoli to the side.

Make It MyPlate:
Add protein and fruit.

Ingredient List:	Equipment List:
broccoli tomatoes pasta sauce pasta (whole wheat) Optional: Bring in various shapes of pasta to teach the names; allow kids to pick their favorite shape!	Measuring cups and spoons Knife Cutting board Microwave Stove top burner Colander Medium pot Cooking spoon Serving spoon Attractive dinner plate **Paper Goods and Misc:** Plates, napkins, and forks for tasting Paper towels for kitchen cleanup Baggies and plastic cups for ingredients Cleaning supplies for kitchen sanitation

Microwave Veggies

Ingredients:
Corn on the cob with light margarine
Broccoli with lemon
Baby carrots with honey
Potatoes with fat-free sour cream

ChooseMyPlate.gov

Directions:
• Husk the corn and wrap in plastic wrap; microwave for 3 minutes per ear. Serve with light margarine.
• Rinse the broccoli and place the tops in a covered dish; microwave on high for 3-4 minutes. Serve with lemon.
• Place the carrots in a microwaveable container; sprinkle with a little water; cover and microwave on high until tender, about 5 minutes. Serve with honey.
• Wash potatoes and pierce with fork. Microwave on high for 4-5 minutes per potato. Serve with fat-free sour cream.

Now kids have 4 different vegetables they can prepare with the microwave!

Ingredient List:	Equipment List:
corn light margarine baby carrots honey broccoli lemon baking potatoes (medium) fat-free sourcream Optional: Compare the fat in different kinds of margarine. Compare the fat in regular versus fat-free sour cream. Compare the sodium in fresh versus canned vegetables.	Measuring cups and spoons Knife Cutting board Microwave Microwave containers Serving spoon Attractive dinner plates **Paper Goods and Misc:** Plates, napkins, and forks for tasting Paper towels for kitchen cleanup Baggies and plastic cups for ingredients Cleaning supplies for kitchen sanitation

Healthy Mac and Cheese

Ingredients:
1 box macaroni and cheese mix
2 tablespoons grated carrot
1/4 cup skim milk
Peas with light margarine

Directions:
Cook macaroni in plenty of boiling water until tender, about 5 minutes. Drain and reserve in colander.

Grate carrot into the same sauce pan. Add the milk and bring to a boil. Lower to simmer for 1 minute and then add the cooked macaroni and half the cheese mix. Serve hot.

Meanwhile, heat the peas and serve on the side.

Make It MyPlate:
This healthier grain needs protein, veggies and fruit.

Ingredient List:	Equipment List:
1 box mac and cheese mix	Measuring cups and spoons
1 carrot	Stove top burner (can use portable one)
Skim milk	Medium pans
Frozen peas	Colander
Light margarine for peas	Grater
	Cooking spoon
Optional: Compare prepared macaroni and cheese mix with this recipe; compare regular milk with skim milk. Make a large salad to go with this dish.	Serving spoon
	Attractive dinner plate
	Paper Goods and Misc:
	Plates, napkins, and forks for tasting
	Paper towels for kitchen cleanup
	Baggies and plastic cups for ingredients
	Cleaning supplies for kitchen sanitation

Pizza

Ingredients:
Whole wheat flour tortillas
Pasta sauce
Assorted fresh veggies
Light mozzarella grated cheese

Directions:
Preheat oven to 350 degrees. Top tortillas with pasta sauce and a variety of fresh veggies - allow everyone to make their own concoction. Sprinkle lightly with light mozzarella cheese. Bake until veggies are heated through and cheese melts, about 10-15 minutes. Serve hot.

Make It MyPlate:
Add protein and fruit.

Ingredient List:	Equipment List:
Whole wheat flour tortillas	Measuring cups and spoons
Pasta sauce (low-sodium)	Knife
Fresh veggies: peppers, onions, mushrooms, tomatoes, green onion	Cutting board
Light mozzarella cheese	Baking pans
	Spatula
	Oven or toaster oven
Optional: Compare frozen pizza to this recipe to save calories, sodium, fat and saturated fat.	Attractive dinner plate
	Paper Goods and Misc:
	Plates, napkins, and forks for tasting
	Paper towels for kitchen cleanup
	Baggies and plastic cups for ingredients
	Cleaning supplies for kitchen sanitation

Stir 'Em Stir Fry

Ingredients:
2 cups cooked brown rice
1 tablespoon oil
1 garlic clove
1 tablespoon grated ginger
4 cups fresh stir fry veggies (broccoli, red pepper, mushrooms, carrots, celery)
2 tablespoons light soy sauce

Directions:
Add oil to a large nonstick skillet (or wok) and heat over medium-high stove. Saute garlic and ginger for about a minute then add the rest of the vegetables. Stir fry til crisp-tender, about 8 minutes. Season with soy sauce and serve over hot cooked rice.

Make It MyPlate:
Add protein and fruit.

Ingredient List:	Equipment List:
Brown rice	Measuring cups and spoons
Canola oil	Knife
Garlic	Cutting board
Ginger	Rice cooker
Assorted fresh veggies: broccoli, red pepper, mushrooms, carrots, celerty	Stove top burner (can use portable one)
Light soy sauce	Nonstick skillet or wok
	Cooking spoon
Optional: Compare brown and white rice. Compare boxed rice mixes to plain rice for sodium content. Compare regular soy sauce to light soy sauce for sodium content.	Serving spoon
	Attractive dinner plate

Paper Goods and Misc:
Plates, napkins, and forks for tasting
Paper towels for kitchen cleanup
Baggies and plastic cups for ingredients
Cleaning supplies for kitchen sanitation

Make Your Own Taco

Ingredients:
2 cups cooked brown rice
1 can pinto beans
Prepared salsa
Fat-free sour cream
Chopped romaine lettuce (washed and ready to serve)
1 cup chopped tomatoes
4 flour tortillas

Directions: Cook rice and set aside; drain pinto beans and heat in microwave. Place salsa, sour-cream, tomatoes and romaine in serving bowls. Warm tortillas in microwave. Place all ingredients in buffet and let everyone make their own soft tacos. If you like, you can also use corn tortilla shells.

Make It MyPlate:
Ad protein and fruit.

Ingredient List:	Equipment List:
Brown rice	Bowls for ingredients
Pinto beans	Can opener
Salsa	Knife
Fat-free sour cream	Cutting board
Romaine lettuce	Rice cooker
Ripe tomato	Stove top burner (can use portable one)
Whole grain flour tortillas	Nonstick skillet
	Cooking spoon
Optional: Compare these tacos with the ones in fast food places like Taco Bell for fat and saturated fat.	Serving spoon
	Attractive dinner plate
Check out the fiber content in pinto beans!	

Paper Goods and Misc:
Plates, napkins, and forks for tasting
Paper towels for kitchen cleanup
Baggies and plastic cups for ingredients
Cleaning supplies for kitchen sanitation

© Food & Health Communications *www.foodandhealth.com*

Salad for Kings and Queens

Ingredients:
Romaine lettuce (ready to serve)
Chopped tomatoes
Sliced peppers
Sliced green onions
Sliced cucumber
Baby carrots
Celery Sticks
Assorted flavored vinegars
Olive oil
Black pepper to taste
Assorted light salad dressings

Directions: Place the romaine lettuce in a large salad bowl. Top with chopped tomatoes, sliced peppers, green onions and cucumbers. Place the baby carrots and celery sticks in a vertical pattern like a king's crown around the edge of the bowl. Serve with assorted vinegars and dressings.

Make It MyPlate:

Add your favorite whole grain, lean protein and fruit.

Ingredient List:	Equipment List:
Romaine lettuce	Salad bowl and tongs
Ripe tomatoes	Knife
Bell pepper	Cutting board
Green onions	Cruet for oil
Cucumber	Attractive dinner plate
Baby carrots	
Celery sticks	**Paper Goods and Misc:**
Flavored vinegar	
Olive oil	Plates, napkins, and forks for tasting
Black pepper	Paper towels for kitchen cleanup
Light dressing	Baggies and plastic cups for ingredients
Optional: Compare various salad dressings versus vinegar for sodium and fat content.	Cleaning supplies for kitchen sanitation

Baked Burgers and Fries

Ingredients:
3 baking potatoes
Cooking oil spray
Turkey burger patties
Lettuce
Tomato
Ketchup (low sodium)
Whole wheat bread

Directions:
Preheat oven to 450 degrees F. Cut potatoes in wedges and place on non-stick baking tray. Spray the top of the potatoes with the cooking spray. Bake until crispy on the bottom side, about 14 minutes then flip over and bake until crispy on the other side, about 5 minutes. Meanwhile, bake the burger patties. Serve the patties with the lettuce, tomato and whole grain bread. Garnish with drizzles of ketchup.

Make It MyPlate:

Add some fruit to the side.

Ingredient List:	Equipment List:
Potatoes	Knife
Cooking oil spray	Cutting board
Turkey burger patties	Oven
Lettuce	Baking trays
Tomato	Spatula
Ketchup (low sodium)	Serving spoon
Whole wheat bread	Attractive dinner plate
Optional: Compare recipe to nutrition facts for fast food burgers and fries.	**Paper Goods and Misc:**
	Plates, napkins, and forks for tasting
	Paper towels for kitchen cleanup
	Baggies and plastic cups for ingredients
	Cleaning supplies for kitchen sanitation

Baked Potato Bar

Ingredients:
4 medium baking potatoes
2 cups broccoli tops
Light margarine
Fat-free sour cream
Diced tomato
Chopped green onion

ChooseMyPlate.gov

Directions: Rinse dirt from potatoes and pierce with a fork. Bake potatoes in microwave for 4-5 minutes per potato. Meanwhile trim and rinse broccoli and place in covered bowl. Cut the tomatoes and green onions and place in bowls. When potatoes come out of the microwave, cook the broccoli in the covered bowl in the micrwave for 3-4 minutes or until tender. Cut the potatoes in half and serve all buffet style - allowing everyone to make their own baked stuffed potato!

Make It MyPlate:
Add protein, grains and fruit.

Ingredient List:	Equipment List:
4 baking potatoes	Knife
1 stalk broccoli	Cutting board
Light margarine	Microwave
Fat-free sourcream	Bowls for ingredients
Ripe tomato	Serving spoons
Green onions	Fork to fluff potato
	Attractive dinner plate
Optional: Compare these potatoes to French fries. Compare light margarine to butter. Compare regular sour cream to fat-free sour cream.	**Paper Goods and Misc:** Plates, napkins, and forks for tasting Paper towels for kitchen cleanup Baggies and plastic cups for ingredients Cleaning supplies for kitchen sanitation

Chicken and Veggie Sticks and Dip

Ingredients:
Chicken tenders, 12 ounces
Barbecue sauce, 3 tablespoons
Baby carrots, 2 cups
Celery sticks, 1 cup
Broccoli tops, 1 cup
Light ranch dip, 1 cup

ChooseMyPlate.gov

Directions: Place chicken tenders in a single layer in a glass microwaveable square baking pan. Lightly drizzle with barbecue sauce and cover with plastic wrap. Microwave on high for 5 minutes. Stir. Microwave until chicken is firm and done and no longer pink in the center, about 8 minutes total. Meanwhile, make a platter with the dip in the center and the raw veggies around it. Serve the hot chicken fingers with the veggies and dip.

Make It MyPlate:
Add a whole grain pita and fruit.

Ingredient List:	Equipment List:
12 oz chicken tenders	Microwave
Barbecue sauce	Knife
Baby carrots	Cutting board
Celery sticks	Baking dish
Broccoli tops	Bowl for dip
Light ranch dip	Serving platter
Optional: Serve with whole grain pita pockets (warmed). Compare this recipe to fried chicken fingers for calories, fat and sodium.	**Paper Goods and Misc:** Plates, napkins, and forks for tasting Paper towels for kitchen cleanup Baggies and plastic cups for ingredients Cleaning supplies for kitchen sanitation

Citrus Fruits

(Navel oranges, tangerines, tangelos, white grapefruit, ruby red grapefruit, lemons, limes, etc)

Nutrition:

Citrus fruits are high in Vitamin C and good sources of folate, dietary fiber, potassium and antioxidants. Pink and red hued fruits such as red grapefruit also provide Vitamin A. They are low in calories and contain no fat or cholesterol. One orange provides more than a full day's requirement of Vitamin C for about 80 calories.

When:

Citrus fruits of one variety or another are available year-round from California, Texas, Florida or Arizona. The peak season for tangerines, tangelos, mandarins and navel oranges is December through February.

Selection and Storage:

Choose fruit that is firm and heavy for its size, blemish-free and sweetly fragrant. Avoid fruits that are bruised or have wrinkled, discolored skins. A slight green color in some oranges is normal. Citrus may be stored at room temperature for a week and in a plastic bag in the refrigerator for up to one month.

Serving Suggestion:

Strawberry Orange Cooler
1 cup low-fat strawberry yogurt
1 teaspoon grated orange peel
1 Tablespoon sugar (optional)
1 seedless orange, peeled and sliced
¾ cup cold skim milk.
Combine all the ingredients in a blender and blend until smooth. Serve immediately. Garnish with a fresh strawberry. Recipe courtesy of the American Dairy Association

Did you know?

Grapefruits can have a negative effect on some medication. Talk with your doctor or pharmacist about other citrus fruits that you can safely consume.

Root Vegetables

(Parsnips, beets, rutabagas, turnips and carrots)

Nutrition:

Root vegetables contain Vitamins C and A and dietary fiber. They are also low in calories.

When:

Most root vegetables mature during late fall and early winter. They can successfully be stored for a long period of time in low temperatures and high humidity, allowing the harvest to be available for many months including deep into winter.

Selection and storage:

Avoid roots that are large as they will be fibrous and woody. Avoid wilted, flabby, rough or shriveled roots. All should be blemish-free. Store root vegetables in a perforated plastic bag in the refrigerator. Parsnips and turnips may be stored 3-4 weeks. Rutabagas may have a wax coating and will keep up to two months (the wax should be pared away before cooking). Beets should be used within two weeks. Carrots taste best when used within two weeks, but will keep their nutritional value for several weeks.

Did you know?

Carrots have more vitamin A than any other vegetable and are rich in potassium and calcium. One cup of cooked carrots contains 45 calories.

Serving suggestion:

Root vegetables may be roasted, steamed, baked, braised or microwaved. Eat cubed or sliced tossed with orange or lemon peel. Mash and season with dill, caraway seed, savory or nutmeg.

By Cheryle Syracuse, MS

Bananas

Nutrition:
Bananas are an excellent source of Vitamin B6 and a good source of fiber, Vitamin C and potassium. They are fat, cholesterol and sodium free. One medium banana contains 110 calories and 3 grams of dietary fiber.

When?
The year round availability of bananas, their relatively low price, ease in storage and packing for lunches or an anytime snack makes this a popular fruit. Most of the bananas in the United States are imported form Central or South America.

Selection and Storage:
Choose firm unbruised fruit with a small amount of green on the peel and stem. Bananas will ripen after they are picked. Do not store in a plastic bag. Keep at room temperature. Bananas are fully ripe when yellow. To slow ripening, store in the refrigerator (the peel will turn black, but the inside will be firm). One pound = 3 bananas =1 cup mashed.

Serving Suggestions:
Bananas may be eaten raw or cooked. Toss with lemon or pineapple juice to keep from turning brown.

By Cheryle Syracuse, MS

Broccoli

Nutrition:
Broccoli is high in Vitamin C and folate. It is a good source of dietary fiber, and potassium. It is low in sodium and fat and cholesterol free. Broccoli belongs to the cabbage family and is a cruciferous vegetable. Cruciferous vegetables contain natural phytochemical compounds that protect against some types of cancers.

When?
Broccoli is available year round. Other closely related vegetables include: broccolini (a cross between broccoli and kale); broccoflower (a cross between broccoli and cauliflower) and broccoli rabe or rapini (medium-sharp green with broccoli-like flowers on long stems with spiky leaves.)

Selection and Storage:
Select those with firm stalks. The leaves and stems of the broccoli should be dark green and the florets should be tight and blue-green. Yellow flowers indicate the broccoli is old. Store broccoli unwashed in a plastic bag in the refrigerator and use within 3-5 days.

Serving suggestion:
Broccoli may be eaten raw or cooked. The florets add color and variety to relish plates or salads. Peel the stems and cut away any tough areas, the stems may be eaten with the florets or chopped and used separately in salads or sliced and steamed or stir-fried. To preserve nutrients cook rapidly until just tender crisp, do not over cook.
Apple Broccoli Salad
2 McIntosh, Empire or Cortland Apples, cored and chopped
2 cups fresh raw broccoli, cut up
¼ cup nuts (walnuts or pecans)
1 Tablespoon onion (red or white) chopped
1/3-cup raisins or dried cranberries
½ cup vanilla low-fat yogurt
Mix all ingredients together and serve on a bed of lettuce. Adapted from the New York Apple Association.

Did you know?
Broccoli has more than twice the vitamin C ounce-for-ounce than oranges?

Tropical Fruit (mangos and papaya)

Nutrition:
These tropical fruits are low in calories/fat andare cholesterol free. They provide dietary fiber, potassium and folate. Both are top sources of cancer-fighting antioxidants. Mangos are high in Vitamin A and a good source of Vitamin C. Papayas are excellent sources of both Vitamins A and C

When?
The melon-like papaya with yellow-orange flesh is extremely perishable with a shelf life of just 3-8 days. They can be grown in Hawaii and Florida and are imported from Central and South American, the Caribbean and Asia. The ripe fruit is usually eaten raw, without the skin or seeds. Slightly green papayas will ripen quickly at room temperature, especially if placed in a paper bag. As the papaya ripens, it will turn from green to yellow. Place ripe papayas in a plastic bag and store in the refrigerator. They will keep for up to a week, but it's best to use them within a day or two. Papaya can be found all year long with the peak season in early summer and fall.

Selection and storage:
Mangos will ripen after harvest. Store at room temperature until ripe. When ripe, mangoes are fully colored from green to yellow, with a red tinge, feel fairly firm when pressed and have a fruity aroma. Avoid fruit that is extremely soft and bruised. When ripe place in a plastic bag in the refrigerator up to 3-4 days. Mangos are grown in tropical climates and mostly imported from Mexico, Central/ South American and the Caribbean. They're available all year.

Serving suggestions:
Both are great combined in a fruit salad. Use mango as you would peaches. The unripe green fruit of papaya can be eaten cooked in curries, salads, chutneys and stews. Ripe papayas are frequenlty served with a spinkle of lime to accent the mild taste.

Greens (spinach, kale, collards, Swiss chard, beet greens, broccoli rabe, mustard greens, turnip greens)

Nutrition:
Leafy green vegetables provide Vitamins A, C and K, calcium, iron, folate, magnesium and fiber. Greens are low sodium and fat and cholesterol free. They are also low in calories: one cup chopped raw spinach has 14 calories and ½ cup cooked collards supplies 38 calories.

When?
Most greens can be grown in cool temperature and some are best harvested after a frost making one variety or another available almost year round. Typically greens are available form early spring until late fall.

Selection and storage:
Look for fresh springy leaves. Avoid greens that are wilted, soft, yellow or dried-out. Younger and smaller leaves are tenderer and less bitter. When selecting greens for cooking, remember they cook down considerably from their original volume. Store wrapped in a damp paper towel in a perforated plastic bag in the refrigerator. Keep the towel moist. Most varieties will keep 5-7 days.

Serving Suggestions:
Wash carefully just before using to removed dirt, grit and insects. Do not use soap. If using for a salad, pat dry or use a salad spinner to remove excess water. Mild-flavored greens such as spinach, kale and chard may be steamed until barely tender. Stronger-flavored greens such as collards, turnip and mustard greens benefit from longer cooking in a seasoned broth. Do not overcook, as they will become gray, mushy and limp. Greens will develop an acidic taste and dull appearance if cooked in aluminum pans.

Did you know?
Kale can be substituted with any green such as spinach, chard or beet greens.

By Cheryle Syracuse, MS

Avocado

Nutrition:
While high in calories compared to other fruits and vegetables, the fat in avocados is primarily the good-for-you monounsaturated fat. Avocados also provide Vitamins E and B6, potassium and fiber and contain phytonutrients that help prevent many chronic diseases. They are cholesterol and sodium free.

When?
The many varieties of avocados available, mostly from California and South America, make them accessible year round.

Selection and Storage:
If planning to use the avocados right away, select those that yield to gentle pressure. If planning to keep for a while, look for firmness. Store at room temperature. Avocados continue to ripen after picked. The Hass variety turns dark green or black when ripe, other varieties keep their light-green color even when ripe. To speed ripening, put avocados in a brown paper bag for 2-5 days. To speed ripening even more, add an apple to the bag. They may be stored in the refrigerator 2 days after ripening. To keep the bright green color after cutting, sprinkle with lime or lemon juice.

Serving suggestion:
Use nutrient rich avocados in place of other fats or spreads in a sandwich or wrap. They also add spark and flavor to salads.

Did you know?
Ounce-per-ounce avocados contain more potassium than bananas (130 mg per ounce in avocado verses 102 mg per ounce in a banana), but also more calories (about 45 calorie an ounce in a avocado verses 25 calories an ounce in a banana).

By Cheryle Syracuse, MS

Asparagus

Nutrition:
Asparagus is an excellent source of folate and Vitamin K and a good source of Vitamin A and Vitamin C. One spear contains only 4 calories.

When?
Prime months for availability include March, April, May and June.

Selection and Storage:
Select asparagus spears with stalks ½" thick or smaller if possible. Avoid buds that have opened. Look for spears that have green at least two-thirds of the way up the spear. To keep moist, cut the bottom ends off and store standing upright in an inch of water in the refrigerator or cover with a wet paper towel and place in a plastic bag in the refrigerator. Use within 2-3 days for best quality. Peel any tough or woody portions of the stalk, especially towards the base. The peeled ends may be saved and used for cream of asparagus soup. Add grated ends and peels to quick breads and cookies.

Serving suggestion:
Asparagus may be eaten raw or cooked. Do not overcook, the spears should remain firm and retain its crunch. Cook fresh asparagus in a small amount of boiling water until tender. Fresh asparagus will be crisp-tender in 5 to 8 minutes. Microwave fresh asparagus by placing one pound in a microwavable baking dish or serving bowl. If cooking whole spears, arrange with tips in center. Add about 1/4-cup water and cover tightly. Microwave at 100% power for 4 to 7 minutes for spears, 3 to 5 minutes for cuts and tips. Stir or turn halfway through cooking time.

For a special treat, grill asparagus with a little olive oil. Lightly coat the spears with oil, grill over high heat for 2- 3 minutes until desired tenderness. Sprinkle with black pepper, lemon pepper or a dash of balsamic vinegar. Serve hot.

Did you know?
Asparagus contains no fat or cholesterol and is naturally very low in sodium.

Berries (strawberries, blueberries and raspberries)

Nutrition:
Strawberries, blueberries and raspberries all contain Vitamin C and fiber. All are fat free, low in calories and have cancer-fighting antioxidants.

Selection and Storage:
Blueberries: Choose firm, plump, dry berries with dusty blue color and uniform in size. They will keep in the refrigerator 10-14 days.

Strawberries: Choose firm berries with a bright red color; they are best if the green leaves are still attached. Avoid shriveled or mushy berries. Refrigerate and use within 1-3 days

Raspberries: Choose firm, plump, dry berries. Avoid wet or moldy berries. Refrigerate and use within 1-2 days.

Do not wash berries until ready to eat.

Serving suggestion:
Combine fresh berries with orange juice and mint leaves for a summer fruit salad.

Did you know?
Strawberries have the most Vitamin C with more than 100% of the recommended daily amount in one cup.

By Cheryle Syracuse, MS

Salad greens (romaine, spinach, radicchio, arugula, escarole, leaf lettuce, iceberg, endive, Boston bib)

Nutrition:
Salad greens are low in calories and sodium and provide color and crunch to a meal. All are fat and cholesterol free. The darker or more colorful the greens, the more nutrients they provide. Varieties such as romaine, leaf lettuces, arugula and spinach are high in Vitamin A and good sources of folate and fiber. Radicchio is high is disease-fighting antioxidants. Some are also good sources of magnesium, calcium and manganese.

Selection and storage:
Avoid greens with brown leaves. The keys to preventing browning during storage are low temperature (ideally 34- 36 degrees) and elimination of excess moisture. It is important that salad greens be well drained before storing. To keep moist, wrap in a damp paper towel and place in a plastic bag in the refrigerator. Use as soon as possible for best quality.

Did you know?
When purchasing bagged salads greens select a "Best if Used by Date" that should give you at least a few days to store after purchased. Do not buy if past that date. Do not purchase greens with a considerable number of brown-edged pieces or if the greens appear excessively wet. Bagged salad greens should be kept in the refrigerator in their original bag. Once opened, store leftovers in the original bag, tightly closed. Most bagged salads are washed and ready-to-eat, read the bag to be sure. It may be washed again, just before use, if desired.

Spinach Berry Pita Pocket
4 cups spinach, washed and torn
1 cup strawberries, hulled and cut in half
1 cup green grapes cut in half
½ cup fat-free Ranch dressing
4 whole-wheat pita pocket bread
¼ cup slivered almonds.
Combine spinach, strawberries and grapes and dressing; mix well. Cut the pita pockets in half and stuff with salad. Sprinkle with almonds. Source: 5-A-Day.

Cherries

Nutrition:
Cherries are fat, cholesterol and sodium free. They are a good source of Vitamin C, fiber and potassium. One cup of cherries provides 100 calories.

Selection and storage:
There are two basic types of cherries: sweet cherries (sold fresh for eating and used to make maraschino cherries) and tart cherries (used for pies, preserves and juice). When selecting fresh cherries, look for smooth skins and attached stems. Avoid soft or shriveled cherries. Store in the refrigerator for up to 10 days. Most Americans eat approximately 2.6 pounds of cherries per year.

When?
Washington, Oregon, California and Michigan are the top cherry producing states with peak season ranging from June till August.

Serving suggestions:
Throw some dried sweet cherries in your breakfast oatmeal. Mix tart cherries with sausage or other ground meats for a tender lower-fat burger or meat loaf. The cherries add flavor and moistness to the meat without extra calories or fat.

Did you know?
Cherry processors have efficient machines that remove the cherry pits without destroying the cherry. Processors even have pit detectors to eliminate as many pits as possible from cherry products.

By Cheryle Syracuse, MS

Tomatoes

Nutrition:
Tomatoes are high in Vitamins A and C and a good source of potassium. They are fat and cholesterol free and low in calories. One medium tomato has only 35 calories. Cooked tomato products also contain lycopene a powerful disease-fighting antioxidant.

Selection and storage:
Tomatoes can be red, orange, orange-pink, or yellow when ripe, depending upon the variety. Tomatoes will continue to ripen after picking. Keep tomatoes on the kitchen counter (tomatoes do not need sunlight to ripen). Do not refrigerate because stops tomatoes' ripening process and affects the flavor. Once fully ripe, store tomatoes in the refrigerator up to two weeks.

Serving suggestion:
For grilled tomatoes place smaller whole tomatoes on skewers and cook on a hot grill until heated through. Serve drizzled with a little olive oil, basil and balsamic vinaigrette.

Make your own salsa:
In a blender or food processor combine tomatoes, onions, green peppers, garlic and jalapeno or hot peppers. Keeps 3-4 weeks in the refrigerator.

Did you know?
Botanically, tomatoes are a fruit. This is because, generally, a fruit is the edible part of the plant that contains seeds, while a vegetable is the edible stem, leaves or roots of the plant. Most people think it is a vegetable, because it is usually eaten like a vegetable as part of the main meal.

Peaches

Nutrition:
Peaches are fat, cholesterol and sodium free. They contain fiber, Vitamins A and C and potassium. Peaches also contain phytonutrients and antioxidants. One medium peach or one cup of sliced peaches has about 60 calories.

Selection and Storage:
Sweetness does not increase after picking, and so it is best to purchase peaches that were picked as ripe as possible. Choose fragrant peaches with firm, fuzzy skins that yield to gentle pressure when ripe. Avoid hard peaches with a greenish color. A reddish color is not a sure sign of ripeness, look for fruit with a creamy to gold under color are indicators of ripeness. Peaches are very perishable, so only buy what you plan to use. Store unripe peaches in paper bag at room temperature. Once ripe, keep peaches at room temperature for use within 1-2 days or in the refrigerator for up to 6 days. Peaches are best eaten at room temperature.
Typically peaches come in "freestone" or "clingstone" varieties. This refers to whether the flesh sticks to the stone (pit) or not. Peaches can have yellow or white flesh.
Peaches will peel easily if placed in boiling water for one minute and then cooled quickly in ice water. To keep cut peaches from turning brown when exposed to air, sprinkle with lemon or lime juice or ascorbic acid.

Did you know?
A nectarine is really a variey of peach with a smooth and shiny skin.

Serving Suggestion:
Whirl ripe peaches in a blender with your favorite iced tea for your own flavored and nutritious version of peach tea. Sweeten to taste and garnish with sliced peaches, mint or ginger.
Add a southern flare to chicken salad by adding ripe diced peaches and chopped pecans.

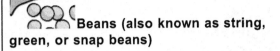

Beans (also known as string, green, or snap beans)

Nutrition:
Beans are fat, saturated fat, cholesterol and sodium free. They are a good source of fiber and Vitamin C and are low in calories.

Selection and Storage:
Snap or green beans are the immature pods of the bean plant; the entire pod can be eaten. If allowed to grow the bean inside will grow larger and can be harvested into fresh beans (or shell beans). For snap beans choose fresh looking beans that snap easily when bent. The pods should be immature with just small beans visible through the pods.

To use, break off the stem end. The pointed end may be eaten or removed. Beans may be cooked whole or broken into bite-size pieces. For shell beans, select beans that are fresh looking. The pods should not be limp or streaked with brown. Select those with mature beans, but not oversized. Huge beans indicate old beans. Refrigerate unwashed in a plastic bag, use within 1 week. Wash beans just before cooking. If using them as shell beans, leave in pods until just before cooking.

For snap beans the size of the pod and the bean determines the cooking time. To cook snap beans, place in boiling water or steam for 3-5 minutes. Beans may be eaten hot or cold.

Serving Suggestion:
To serve cold in a salad immediately plunge the hot beans into cold or ice water to stop the cooking. For a crisp bean salad: toss cooked and cooled beans with sliced green or red onions and olive oil and lemon juice or a vinaigrette dressing.

By Cheryle Syracuse, MS

© Food & Health Communications *www.foodandhealth.com*

Melons (watermelon, muskmelons)

Nutrition:

All melons are low in calories, fat and cholesterol and are sodium free.

- *Muskmelons* varieties include both cantaloupe and honeydews. Orange cantaloupes contain very high amounts of Vitamins A and C as well as potassium, calcium, folate and iron. Honeydew melons are an excellent source of Vitamin C and modest amounts of potassium but almost no Vitamin A.

- *Watermelon* is a good source of Vitamins A and C. Watermelon also provides vitamin B6 and potassium. Pink watermelon contains the potent carotenoid antioxidant, lycopene, having higher concentrations of lycopene than any other fresh fruit or vegetable, including tomatoes.

Selection and Storage:

- Ripe cantaloupes have a sweet musky smell, yield to pressure on the blossom end and have a yellowish cast under the raised netting.

- As honeydew melons ripen, the outside rind turns from green to creamy white to yellow. A creamy white melon will ripen at room temperature in a few days. Muskmelons should be held at room temperature until they ripen.

- As a watermelon ripens, the ground spot changes from pale green or white to cream or yellow. The tendrils near the fruit stem will dry and turn brown. The sound of a watermelon, when thumped with a finger, is a muffled, dull tone if it is ripe. An immature fruit will thump with a clear, metallic ringing tone. When selecting a cut watermelon, the more red flesh and less white rind, the riper the melon.

Once cut, store all melon in a tightly closed container as its aroma easily mingles with other foods. Cut slices or chunks of melon should never be left out or held at room temperature for an extended period of time. Use cut melon within 3-4 days.

By Cheryle Syracuse, MS

Did you know?

Bacteria can adhere to the surface of a melon. The melon's skin should be washed and scrubbed with water even if you don't eat the rind or skin.

Serving suggestions:

Top cubes of melon with low-fat fruit yogurt and sprinkle with granola for a quick breakfast.

Sweet Corn

Nutrition:

Sweet corn is low in fat, saturated fat, cholesterol and sodium free. One medium ear provides 10% of the recommended needed Vitamin C. Yellow sweet corn provides some Vitamin A. One cooked ear of corn contains 85 calories.

Selection and Storage:

Select corn that has green husks, fresh silks and ears with well-filled bright colored, milky kernels. The stems of freshly picked corn will be damp and pale green. Avoid yellow or dried husks. When selecting sweet corn, pull back the husks and silk, the ears should be free of insect and disease. Because the sugar loss is rapid at high temperatures, corn should be cooled as quickly as possible. Sweet corn can be stored in refrigeration from 5-7 days and the sweeter varieties up to 12 days.

Corn can be eaten directly from the cob or cut off the cob. Corn-on-the cob may be boiled in unsalted water (4-8 minutes depending upon size or ears) or microwaved whole covered (with either the husks or plastic wrap) for 3 minutes per ear.

Did you know?

Corn can be found in more than 3,000 products on the grocery shelf. Corn has many uses: corn sweetener, corn oil, cornstarch, corn syrup and eaten "as is."

Serving suggestion:

Toss canned black beans (drained), chopped tomatoes and roasted corn kernels with salsa for a quick Mexican salad. To roast corn, remove silk but leave the husks on the ears, soak in water for 10 minutes. Place on in a 375-degree oven for 20-30 minutes or on a grill for 15-20 minutes, turning occasionally.

Grapes

Nutrition:

Grapes supply small amounts of potassium, thiamin, phosphorous, and Vitamin A. They are fat and cholesterol free, very low in sodium and low in calories. Ten grapes contain about 40 calories and grape juice contains about 165 calories per cup.

Recent studies show that grapes are rich in several phytonutrients that help prevent certain types of cancers and heart disease. The skins of all colors of grapes contain the antioxidant resveratrol, a phytonutrient that has anti-inflammatory and cancer fighting properties. These antioxidants can be found in fresh grapes, grape juices and wine.

Grapes grow in clusters and can range in color from crimson, black, dark blue, yellow, green to pink. Most of the world's grape harvest is made into wine, but 27% is used as fresh fruit and 2% as dried fruit (raisins). Other uses include grape juice, jams and jellies.

Selection and Storage:

Grapes do not ripen after they are picked. Grapes should be firm, plump, well colored, and firmly attached to pliable stems. Avoid grapes that are shriveled or soft at the stem. Moldy and wet grapes indicate decay. Buy only the amount of grapes can use up in a short period of time. Seedless table grapes are the most popular for fresh eating. Grapes will keep in a plastic bag in the refrigerator for up to one week but are best when eaten within two to three days. Wash grapes just before serving by holding under cool running water.

Did you know?

Unpasteurized grape juice may contain bacteria that make children, older adults, and those with weakened immune systems sick. If someone in your family is at high-risk and you cannot determine if a juice product has been pasteurized to destroy harmful bacteria, either don't use it or bring it to a boil to kill any possible harmful bacteria.

Serving Suggestion:

Freeze washed grapes and pop them in your mouth while still frozen. Add fresh grapes to any salad for a change of pace.

Summer Squash and Zucchini

Nutrition:

Zucchini and summer squash are a good source of vitamins A and C and potassium. They are mostly water and low in calories with only about 15 calories per ½ cup. They do not contain any fats, saturated fats, sodium or cholesterol.

Selection and storage:

Select firm and blemish free zucchini and summer squash that are no larger than 4-6 inches long and about 1 to 2" aground. Avoid withered or limp-looking squash. Larger squash are tough and full of seeds. Store in a perforated plastic bag in the refrigerator. Do not wash until ready to eat. They are best if used within 4 to 5 days. As the name suggests, these tender squash have peak availability during the hot summer months.

Did you know?

Zucchini is a summer squash. Others include yellow crookneck, yellow straight neck and scalloped patty pan squash. In most recipes, all summer squash are interchangeable.

Serving suggestions:

Do not overcook zucchini or summer squash the result will be mush! There is no need to peel or seed young tender squash. Zucchini and summer squash can be in raw in salad or with a dip. Summer squash should be harvested in the young immature state and the skins and seeds are eaten. Larger squash can be peeled, seeded and grated and used cooked in items such as muffins, breads or casseroles.

By Cheryle Syracuse, MS

Apples

Nutrition:
Apples contain small amounts of Vitamins A and C, thiamin, iron and calcium. Apples are a good source of both soluble and insoluble dietary fiber. One medium apple provides approximately 75 calories.

Selection and Storage:
Select firm apples with no signs or bruises, decay, broken or shriveled skin. Store apples in a perforated plastic bag in the refrigerator. They should keep up to three weeks.

Did you know?
Eating an apple with the skin gives you more nutrition. Almost ½ of the vitamin C content is just beneath the skin.

Serving Suggestions:
Add cored and cut up apples to Cole slaw for added sweetness and color. Cut up pecans add additional crunch.

Apple Slaw
1 apple, cored and chopped
4 cups shredded cabbage
1/2 cup chopped red onions
1 sweet pepper, chopped
1/2 cup nonfat vanilla yogurt
2 Tbsp orange juice
pinch cinnamon
Directions:
Combine all ingredients in mixing bowl and serve chilled. Serves 4. Each serving: 1 cup.

By Cheryle Syracuse, MS

Cabbage (green head cabbage, red cabbage, Savoy cabbage, Napa or Chinese cabbage)

Nutrition:
Cabbage is high in vitamin C, low in calories and very low in sodium. It contains no fat or cholesterol. Cabbage family (cruciferous) vegetables are particularly powerful cancer fighters. An optimal diet includes several servings of the cabbage or other cruciferous vegetables per week. Red cabbage is four times higher in these protective compounds than green cabbage

Selection and Storage:
Choose firm heads that feel heavy for their size. The outer leaves should look fresh, have good color and be free of blemishes. Refrigerate, unwashed, in plastic bag for up to one week. Use Napa cabbage within 4 days. For head cabbages, pull off and discard any wilted outer leaves before use.

Did you know?
When cabbage is cut or crushed it begins to loose its Vitamin C. You can save the Vitamin C by cutting the cabbage just before serving, and then add the dressing at once. The acid in the dressing helps to protect the Vitamin C.

Serving suggestion:
Apples and Cabbage
1 large onion, chopped
1 Tablespoon vegetable oil
1-pound cabbage (about ½ head)
2 apples (Jonathan, Jonagold, Granny Smith or Gala)
¼ teaspoon black pepper
1 Tablespoon brown sugar
1-cup warm water or apple juice
1 Tablespoon apple cider vinegar
Dash nutmeg
Wash, core and thinly slice the cabbage and apples. In large skillet sauté onions in the oil until tender. Add the cabbage and apples, cover and cook for 5 minutes. Add the rest of the ingredients to the cabbage and cook, covered, over low heat for 20 minutes, stirring occasionally. Can be served hot or cold. Serves 6.

Cranberries

Nutrition:

Cranberries are high in fiber and vitamin C and contain just 25 calories per 1/2 cup of fresh berries. They are also low in sodium and are a source of Vitamins A & B, calcium, phosphorus, and iron. Packed full of antioxidants and other natural compounds, cranberries promote the prevention of urinary tract infections, gum disease and stomach ulcers.

Selection and storage:

Fresh whole cranberries are available in markets from September through December. These berries will keep in the refrigerator for one month. Freezing the berries will make them last all yearlong. White berries are safe to eat; they have just not developed their full color. Sort out any bruised berries and store in an airtight freezer container. These berries do not need to be thawed, but should be washed just before use. Frozen berries will maintain their quality for 9-12 months. Sweetened dried cranberries will keep for up to 12 months in a cool dry place.

Serving suggestions:

Unlike other fruits, cranberries are usually considered too tart to eat alone and are combined with other ingredients to make them palatable. Most cranberry juices have sweeteners added and dried cranberries are sweetened prior to drying. For nutritional and taste boost add dried cranberries to your tossed salads. Add dried cranberries to your breakfast oatmeal or add to your favorite cookie recipe.

By Cheryle Syracuse, MS

Winter Squash or Pumpkins

Nutrition:

Most orange colored squash and pumpkins are an excellent source of beta-carotene, an antioxidant that converts to Vitamin A in the body. Winter squash and pumpkin also have some B vitamins, Vitamin C, iron, calcium and fiber.

Selection and storage:

Winter squash and pumpkins are members of the gourd family and are available for harvest primarily September, October and November. When purchasing pumpkins be sure to select a "sugar" or "pie pumpkin" not a jack-o-lantern pumpkin. These are small with dark flesh inside and are not too stringy and perfect for pies, soups, cookies and puddings. The rinds of pumpkins and other winter squash should be hard and heavy for their size. Avoid pumpkin or squash with cracks or sunken, moldy or soft spots. Store whole in a cool area (50-60 degrees). They will keep for several months if mature and the stem is attached.

Did you know?

Pumpkin has only 80 calories per cup and over 300 % of the recommended daily amount of Vitamin A.

Serving Suggestion:

To make mashed or pureed pumpkin or squash: cut in half and discard seeds and stringy insides. Place the vegetable cut side down in a baking dish. Bake covered with foil in a 375-degree oven for about 1 ½ hour or covered with plastic wrap in a microwave on high for about 7 minutes per pound. After cooking, scoop out the flesh and puree in a food processor or mash with a potato masher. Mashed pumpkins or squash can be eaten as a vegetable side dish, soups, added to breads or muffins or as in desserts, puddings and pies.

Pears

Nutrition:

Pears are an excellent source of dietary fiber and a good source of Vitamin C. They are fat, cholesterol and sodium free. A medium sized pear provides 6 grams of fiber -that's 24% of the recommended daily value and 100 calories. The peel of a pear also contains valuable phytonutrients.

Selection and Storage:

Pears are one of the few fruits that do not ripen successfully on the tree. They are usually harvested when mature, but not ripe. Choose pears that are bright and fresh looking with no bruises. Bartlett pears will change color as they ripen. Pears ripen from the inside out. When ripe the fruit will give gently to gentle pressure near the stem. Store unripe pears at room temperature in a fruit bowl or brown paper bag. Once ripe, place in the refrigerator. The cool temperatures will slow down the ripening process, but won't stop it. Ripe pears will keep in the refrigerator for 3-5 days. Pears absorb and give off odors, so they are best stored away from other produce.

Serving Suggestion:

Crunchy Pears
3 pears
¾ cup water
4 Tablespoons oatmeal
1 Tablespoon sugar
½ teaspoon cinnamon
1 Tablespoon butter.
Cut pears in half and core. Place cut side up in a shallow baking dish. Combine oatmeal, sugar, cinnamon and butter until crumbly. Fill the centers of the pears with the oatmeal mixture. Add water to the bottom of the baking dish. Cover with foil and bake 350 degrees for about 30 minutes.

White and Sweet Potatoes

Nutrition:

Both white and sweet potatoes are low in sodium and fat free. White potatoes contain Vitamin C, thiamin, niacin, iron, potassium and fiber. Sweet potatoes are loaded with carotenoids, one sweet potato provides over 500% of the daily needed about of Vitamin A and 120 calories. Both store well and are available year round while the peak season for sweet potatoes is August through December.

Selection and storage:

Select potatoes that are clean, firm and smooth and with a regular shape so there won't be much waste when peeling. Avoid wilted, wrinkled skins and soft dark areas. Pick sweet potatoes with a deep orange color and avoid those with any sign of decay. Do not refrigerate any potatoes. Keep potatoes in a cool dry well ventilated place. White potatoes will keep longer than sweet potatoes. White potatoes will turn dark once peeled, to prevent this, toss with an ascorbic acid mixture or lemon juice. Soaking for a long time in water will cause nutrient loss.

Did you know?

Green potatoes are actually sunburned. Avoid exposing white potatoes to light (both artificial or natural light). This causes them to turn green. The greening gives potatoes a bitter flavor and should be cut off before cooking.

Serving Suggestion:

Double baked potatoes: cut a baked potato in half. Scoop the insides into a bowl and mash with ¼ cup shredded cheese and 2 Tablespoons skim milk. Spoon the mixture back into the skins. Warm in a microwave for 2 minutes on high. Additional "mix-in" options: cooked broccoli or spinach or sliced green onions.

By Cheryle Syracuse, MS

CPSIA information can be obtained
at www.ICGtesting.com
Printed in the USA
LVOW04s1619280917
550415LV00002B/23/P